DEFEATING & BEATING

depression

the blues

About the Book

It has been said that depression is "the common cold of mental illness." This book was written because of the large number of adolescents the author sees, in her role as a professional counselor, who suffer severe depression but who take no medication for it because of the medications' troublesome side effects. The book sets forth many specific actions which sufferers can take to rid themselves of the debilitating effects of both chronic fatigue syndrome and various levels of depression.

This is not a clinical book—it is a self-help book. It doesn't take the place of a professional counselor, physician or psychiatrist, but it tells everything the author wants her clients, students and readers to know about overcoming Depression, Chronic Fatigue Syndrome, Epstein-Barr Virus and Candida. It is loaded with useful information!

This powerful book is based on the extensive experience and training of the author—a licensed professional counselor who is the President of the Utah Mental Health Counselors' Association. She is a counselor in the Utah public schools, and a Ph.D. candidate in nutrition and natural healing, as well as a holder of a Bachelor's degree in public relations and journalism and a Masters degree in Education.

She writes with flare, verve and gusto. She writes with knowledge and insight. She writes as a crusader who is fighting to overcome the misery and despair which accompany these widespread afflictions. She approaches the problems from a variety of viewpoints, and she brings relief and renewal to many who accept her wisdom. This truly is a valuable, much needed book!

Defeating depression & Beating the blues

A Holistic, Nutritional and Spiritual Approach

Pat Webb, M.Ed., LPC

Horizon Publishers
Springville, Utah

Copyright © 1999, 2004
by HORIZON PUBLISHERS

All rights reserved.

No part of this book may be reproduced in any form whatsoever, whether by graphic, visual, electronic, film, microfilm, tape recording, or any other means, without prior written permision of the author, except in the case of brief passages embodied in critical reviews and articles.

Published by
Horizon Publishers
A division of Cedar Fort Inc.
www.cedarfort.com

v. 3 November 2004

ISBN: 0-88290-664-x

Horizon Publishers' Catalog and Order Number:
C1254

Printed and distributed
in the United States of America by

& Distributors, Incorporated

Address:
925 North Main Street
Springville, Utah 84663

Local Phone: (801) 489-4084
Toll Free: 1 (800) SKYBOOK
FAX: (800) 489-1097

E-mail: horizonp@burgoyne.com
Internet: http://www.horizonpublishersbooks.com

Contents

About the Book 2
Dedication 10
Preface 11
1. In the Belly of the Whale:
   My Experience with the Effects of Severe Depression 13
    My Husband's Death 13
    A Traumatic Birth 13
    A Severe Allergic Reaction 14
    A Loss of Spiritual Strength 15
    Guilt and Grief 15
    Anger 15
    Trapped 16
    Emotional Healing and a Support Group 16
2. If You Feel Suicidal 19
    Call for Help 19
    Nutritional Supplements 19
    Be Active 20
    Control Your Thoughts 20
3. What Is Depression? 23
    The Diagnostic Definition 23
    Different Forms of Depression 24
    Many Causes of Depression 25
    Other Illnesses with Depression Symptoms 25
    Medication-induced Depression 26
    Depression Caused by Life Events 26
    Don't Make Depression a Permanent Guest 26

4. Using Nutritional Supplements and Foods to Fight Depression 27
    Eating Affects Our Moods and Feelings 27
    Neurons and Neurotransmitters. 27
    Amino Acids Regulate Behavior 28
    Prescription Antidepressants 29
    Homeopathic Remedies 30
    Kinesiology Muscle Testing 31
    Hypoglycemia and Sugar Problems 33
    Candida Albicans and Depression 35
    Types of Depression and Their Nutritional Relationships 37

5. Instantaneous Activities that Help Fight Depression. 39

6. Developing a Support System 45
    Easing Other's Burdens Through Support Groups. 45
    Five Categories of Helping Behavior 47
    Your Spiritual Support System 48
    God May Have a Better Plan than We Have. 49

7. Utilize the Power of Positive Self-talk and Affirmations 51
    Our Thoughts Determine Our Feelings and Actions. 51
    What We think About Actually Comes into Our Life 51
    A Technique for Shoving Negative Thoughts Aside 52
    Create Your Own Affirmations 52
    Affirmation Samples 53

8. Conquering Anger. 57
    Anger Can Cause Depression and Inner Turmoil 57
    Cold Anger 57
    Suppressing Anger 58
    Even Nice People Feel Anger 59
    Classifying Your Provocations 60
    Warm Anger. 60
    Techniques for Releasing Your Anger 62

9. Overcoming Guilt ... 65
Unloading the Guilt Bag of Unnecessary Cargo ... 65
Healthy or Unhealthy Guilt? ... 65
Techniques for Releasing Guilt ... 67

10. Vanquishing Fear ... 69
The Escalating Process: From Negative Self-talk
   to Worry to Fear ... 69
Good and Bad Fear ... 70
Instead of "Awfulizing," Try "Positizing" ... 70
Fear Leads to Distrust ... 71

11. Managing Stress ... 75
The Physical Results of Stress ... 75
Take Positive Steps to Reduce Stress ... 75
   Visualization ... 76
   Deep Breathing ... 76
   Progressive Relaxation ... 78
   Exercise ... 79
Gaining Control of Your Time and Your Life ... 79
Secrets of a Good Night's Sleep ... 80
   Mindfulness ... 81
   Yoga ... 83
Keep a Gratitude Journal ... 85
Learned Optimism ... 86

12. Connecting With Your Higher Power ... 89
Help Is Available from On High ... 89
Reach for the Light! ... 90
Aid in Being Restored to Wholeness ... 91
Prayers Are Often Answered through Others ... 93
Blessings Come From Service to Others ... 93
Turning Your Problems over to God ... 94

13. Enduring and Persevering ... 97
Life's Journey: "Hang Ups and Bang Ups" ... 97
The Joy of Life Is the Trip ... 98
We're Here to See One Another Through ... 99
Avoid Self-Pity and Self-Contempt ... 100
Press On ... 101

14. Developing Personal Power 103
Defining Assertive Behavior 103
The Need for Personal Balance 103
Using "I" Messages 105
Using the One-to-ten Scale 106
Passive Individuals 106
Aggressive Individuals 107
Practice Role Playing 107
Three Parts of a Good Assertive Message 108
Avoid Victim Language 108
Moving from Pessimism to Optimism 109
Being Centered and Maintaining Balance 109
Responding to Criticism 111

15. Using Humor as a Healing Tool 113
This Chapter's Messages: The Many Advantages of Humor. . 113
Time Changes Perceptions 114
If You Can Laugh, You Can Survive 115
The Physical Results of Laughter 117

16. Fighting Chronic Fatigue Syndrome,
Epstein-Barr Virus and Candida 121
A Search for Healing of Chronic Fatigue 121
Renewal in California 124
Encountering Kindred Spirits 124
Chronic Fatigue Symptoms 125
Recommended Readings Related to Chronic Fatigue 126
Check for Parasites 127
Recommendations for Fighting Epstein-Barr Virus
   and Candida 128
Cleansing the Colon and Intestinal Tract 129
Main Homeopathic Remedies
   for Chronic Fatigue Syndrome 133
Additional Sources of Help in Fighting CFS and EBV 135
Recuperate Patiently and Positively 135
Increase Your Emotional Altitude Each Day 136
Measure Your Goal Accomplishment 136

17. Homeopathic Remedies for Depression **139**
    Homeopathy Defined 139
    Treating the Whole Person and Each Person Individually . . . 140
    Homeopathic Remedies for Various Types of Depression . . . 140

Bibliography. **145**

Index **147**

About the Author **157**

Dedication

To those who have empowered me;
my thanks. To those I've empowered:
Keep flying, you are the wind beneath my wings.
To my higher power, my eternal gratitude.

Preface

This is not a clinical book, it is a self-help book, and is not intended to take the place of a professional counselor, physician, or psychiatrist. The book is everything I would like my clients to know about overcoming depression, the blues, or anxiety.

Kites rise highest against the wind. Sometimes my greatest tribulations have been my greatest motivators. Like Phoenix rising from the ashes, I've had to pick myself up and go on. As a child, I was sexually abused and lived with alcoholism and poverty. Later in life, and with the help of holistic medicine, I battled Chronic Fatigue Syndrome, then liver cancer—successfully. When I was thirty-three my first husband died. I wanted to die too, but there are many things I would not have accomplished if I had remained in my secure little world. Later, I remarried and divorced.

Adversity can teach people to be strong . . . I gained strength from walking against the wind. I wouldn't have started a support group for single women, finished my bachelor's and master's degree, or presently be a Ph.D. candidate in Nutrition and Natural Healing, nor been a coordinator of a women's center, counseled hundreds of people, worked with youth, or written this book.

I would not have gained the empathy for others that I now have or the philosophy that no matter what happens to you, you can go on from where you are and grow.

Nearly every week I receive calls from someone needing help or wanting to counsel a friend or relative who is suffering from anxiety, depression, the blues, or a mood disorder. This is why I have written this book. It is simple enough for anyone to understand, and it embraces my experience in traditional therapy and my training in nutritional healing. My hope is that it will empower those who need counseling, and that it also will instruct and inspire those who want to help others.

1
In the Belly of the Whale:
My Experience with the Effects of Severe Depression

*For God has not given us the spirit
of fear; but of power, and of love,
and of a sound mind.*

—2 Timothy 1:7

My Husband's Death

Long before I was ever a therapist, I suffered severe depression. I felt as if I had been sucked into the belly of the whale, with no way out. The depression struck after the death of my first husband, Ray, who died of cancer. At the time, we were eagerly expecting our fourth child. We had ten-year-old and seven-year-old sons and a tiny daughter who was two-and-a half. For several months after his death I was emotionally stable, maybe in shock, but definitely sustained by a higher power. It was after the birth of our baby that the black shroud of depression gripped me in a death lock.

A Traumatic Birth

On the 24th of July weekend, a holiday in Utah, I went into labor. It was two months to the day after Ray died. Everyone was out of town, including my doctor, who had been a source of strength to me. My mother lived in Wyoming, my mother-in-law was vacationing in California, my sister was camping, as was my best friend who had planned to take me to the hospital. Mentally I reviewed a list of other friends and family members who were all out of town. Again, I felt abandoned and alone, just as I had when Ray died.

When my pains were five minutes apart, I called my doctor. My pediatrician, who was on call at the clinic, demanded that I go to the hospital. "How many babies have you delivered?" I asked.

"One," he joked. Fortunately, he was not the doctor on call.

Because I felt so alone, I didn't want to go to the hospital, but I couldn't stop the labor pains. Having a baby is something a husband and wife do together, but Ray was gone. Shari, our two-year-old, was howling fearfully. Her strawberry blonde curls wet with tears; she clung to me, afraid to let me leave, terrified that I might not return again, just like her father. Whenever we got into the car, she would ask, "Are we going to find my Daddy?"

A Severe Allergic Reaction

Fortunately, one neighbor was in town and nervously drove me to the hospital. In the labor room the doctor broke my water to speed up delivery. I delivered so fast that I went into shock. My blood felt like ice water; I was shaking all over. Nurses started piling warm blankets on top of me. My doctor administered a shot of Demerol and within a few minutes I was berserk. I ranted and raved most of the night, not remembering that I had delivered a baby girl. I drifted in and out of consciousness. Two nurses watched over me and held me down because I kept trying to get out of bed and leave the hospital. I continually repeated Ray's vital signs which he had just before he died. I knew them well because I took care of him at home throughout his illness. He died in our bed.

As I was coming out of this quagmire of darkness, I recall being at the end of a long, long tunnel, and in the distance was a warm, caring, spiritual person who emanated light and love.

By noon, I had sobered up and was fairly lucid when my parents came to see me. The doctor told them I had likely suffered a mental breakdown and might not ever recover. I was exhausted and deeply depressed. Nurses had ignored my request to see the baby. When they refused to bring her to me I walked to the nursery with my parents. A note attached to her crib said, *Do not take to mother.* She was a beautiful baby with dark eyes, chubby cheeks and black hair, but I was so emotionally (and probably physically) malnourished that I couldn't experience the joy of this tiny little miracle.

By late afternoon, the doctor realized that I was allergic to Demerol. In a few days they released me to go home, but at home the depression did not lift. My candle flickered, but my light within was dim.

A Loss of Spiritual Strength
The spiritual strength that had sustained me during Ray's months of illness had faded. Many times I wanted to die. Why couldn't we have all died together? Why did he have to leave our family? More and more I thought of suicide and ways to do it.

Friends encouraged me by saying, "Count your blessings. You have four beautiful children." This made me feel even more depressed.

Guilt and Grief
Guilt engulfed me because I knew I had blessings but I didn't feel happy, I felt as if I were drowning and being sucked into a whirlpool, reaching my hand up for help, but there was no one there to help me. I felt numb and wooden-hearted. Grief was like a black hole that was eating me up.

Because my suicidal ideation increased, I finally sought help. In therapy I learned that depression can be caused by chemical imbalance, a change in hormones that can happen after the birth of a baby, anger you turn in on yourself, guilt, and feeling trapped. All of these fit me.

Anger
It was difficult to acknowledge that I was angry with Ray for dying and leaving us—especially the children. He had been a marvelous and involved father, and no one could take his place. It didn't seem logical that I could be so angry and blame Ray for dying, because he didn't want to die. As he battled cancer he apologized to

me over and over again, saying "Pat, I didn't know when I married you that this was going to happen. I don't want to leave you and the children."

Now that I understand that most anger is a mask for other feelings, and that it usually arises in response to loss (loss of love, loss of control, and loss of self-esteem) or emotional pain, it makes perfect sense. Also, I found out I was angry with God for letting Ray die; this made me feel very guilty. How could anyone be angry with God? In addition, I felt guilty that my children didn't have a father and felt that he had been a better parent than I.

Trapped

I felt incredibly trapped. I couldn't bring Ray back, and I didn't want to be single or be a single parent.

It took a year to overcome the depression, but identifying my feelings and realizing they were normal, helped me overcome the terrifying feeling of being sucked down into a whirlpool. I learned that I could function on my own, especially with the help of a higher power. My refrigerator motto was, "Two people can do anything as long as one of them is the Lord."

Emotional Healing and a Support Group

As I started to heal emotionally, I used my pain and loneliness to start a support group for other women who were widowed or divorced. Over the years, more than 200 women have been involved in the group and gained strength from each other.

Now, I realize there are other things that could have helped me overcome the suicidal feelings more rapidly. Homeopathy, nutritional supplements, the right kind of food, exercise, yoga, deep breathing, a good support system, and humor—each would have helped me.

Nevertheless, I have gained great empathy for those who grieve, for those who are depressed, and for those who feel as if they are in the belly of the whale. My experience has led me on an unexpected journey to become a therapist (I wanted to be a writer) and, more recently, has led me in my passionate pursuit of a doctoral degree in Nutrition and Natural Healing.

I believe that our total body—mind, spirit, and physical being—is involved in good mental health.

Over the years I have counseled thousands of people who were depressed, and have watched, with gratitude, healing come into their lives.

*When we do the best we can,
we never know what miracle is wrought
in our life, or in the life of another.*

—Helen Keller

2
If You Feel Suicidal

*For every problem under the sun,
there is a remedy or there is none;
if there be one, hurry and find it;
if there be none, never mind it.*

Call for Help

If you have a plan to commit suicide and know how you're going to do it, call your doctor or county mental health crisis line immediately. Most hospitals have crisis workers who are available to talk to you on the phone. Call a counselor, your doctor, a relative, a friend, your religious leader, or a neighbor—someone who can help you. Don't be alone.

Nutritional Supplements

Nutritional supplements and certain foods can alter or help your mood. Dr. Carl C. Pfeiffer, an orthomolecular physician who did psychiatric research for more than thirty years and treated more than 25,000 mentally ill patients successfully with nutrition, states that Vitamin C and niacin (in dosages that provide a mild blushing sensation) provide almost instant relief to the overactive mind and help focus mental concentration. If you have never taken niacin, I suggest taking 25 milligrams and gradually increasing it. Five-hundred mgs. of Vitamin C would be a good start. I would not take more than 300 mg. of niacin a day and I would have someone else in charge of all supplements until the crisis passes.

If you are agitated or feel extreme anxiety, chamomile tea has a calming effect. (Don't take this if you are allergic to ragweed.) Also, bananas or avocados help increase serotonin levels and can relax or calm you down.

Dr. Julian Whitaker's prescription for anxiety includes the homeopathic L.72 Anti-Anxiety formula, 20 drops in 2 to 3 ounces of water, taken three to four times daily, plus 750 to 1,000 milligrams of GABA (an amino acid with a natural calming effect).

Be Active

Women are twice as likely to be depressed as men, because women tend to ruminate or mull things over in their mind more often than men do. When a man is melancholy he usually takes action by going jogging, fishing, playing basketball or going to the gym and working out. Taking action, even if it's cleaning house or briskly walking through a shopping mall, will help depression. Movement is better than sitting still.

Control Your Thoughts

Remember:

- Suicidal thoughts usually last only a short time, sometimes minutes, or a few hours. Now is not forever.

- Take your depressed thoughts with a grain of salt. Depression makes you feel hopeless, worthless, and useless. Recognize that these feelings are the depression talking and that they do not represent the way life is, or who you are.

- Drugs and alcohol make depression worse. Alcohol is a depressant. If you're using either, give them up for a week or ten days until you are through the crisis. There are some herbs or homeopathic remedies that can help you with withdrawal from drugs and alcohol.

- The famed psychiatrist, Dr. Karl Menninger, was once asked what he would advise a person who came to you and said, "I think I'm going to have a nervous breakdown." The psychiatrist answered, "Perhaps most of us would say, go see a psychiatrist." But Menninger said, "Close your house, walk down to the railway tracks, cross them, and find someone in need. Then respond to that need."

- *Return From Tomorrow*, a book about life-after-death experiences describes a young man who had an out-of- body or near death experience. He encountered people who had committed suicide and watched them as they repeatedly approached their relatives who were still on this earth and said, "I'm sorry I did it," over and over again. He saw that they couldn't get through to their mortal relatives, who couldn't hear them. The observer saw that those who committed suicide felt incredible remorse and pain for their act.
- Remember, these feelings will pass.
- Ask yourself: What are you angry about? With whom are you angry? Are you turning that anger in on yourself?
- Write a note or letter to the person you are angry with; you don't have to deliver the note, but getting your feelings out will help.
- If you feel trapped, ask yourself: What are your positive options?
- Ask yourself: Is guilt or an overly-strong conscience driving your depression?
- Exercise, take a brisk walk
- Loudly sing a positive song
- Take a shower
- Dance to some lively music
- Find a meaning in your life that's bigger than yourself, a way to help others.
- Turn, in this book, to the chapter on *Instantaneous Activities That Help*, and browse through the pages. The ideas will help to divert your attention from negative or "stinking thinking" to positive energy.
- Draw a page full of "smiley" faces while you say "Cheese." University studies have proven that using the smile muscles in the face enhances positive endorphins in the brain and body.
- Try placing your hands over your eyes so that you are looking out the extreme right side of your eye. Next, place your palms

over your eyes so your peripheral view is from the extreme left side of your eye. Determine which is more comfortable. In his book, *Of Two Minds*, a Boston physician, Dr. Harvey Schiffer, discovered that by placing tape over goggles so that peripheral vision was accessed either through the extreme right or left eye, depression could be decreased for thirty percent of his depressed patients. That's about the same rate of success as Prozac, but without the side effects of the drug. When they did brain mapping, they actually found that it changed the brain chemistry of the clients.

The good news is that the problems you face now will likely pass. Help is available, and you can help yourself.

Your assignments for this chapter:
1. Start a daily gratitude journal and write down five things that you are grateful for each day. They can be as simple as, "I am grateful for windmills," or "I'm thankful for tooth paste and indoor toilets."

2. Memorize and repeat these positive affirmations:
- I enjoy being happy.
- I am a clear channel for positive thinking.
- I now release all blocked energy.
- I now release all depression and replace it with exhilaration.

3
What Is Depression?

*You cannot prevent the birds of sadness
from flying over your head,
but you can keep them
from nesting in your hair.*

The Diagnostic Definition

Like Jonah, we sometimes end up in the belly of the whale. At least, that's what it feels like. When life kicks you in the gut, wallops you on the jaw, or knocks you for a loop, how do you handle it? How do you know if you're really depressed, or just experiencing a low mood, or just feeling the blues?

Some people feel temporarily blue or depressed because of things such as sadness, grief, divorce, health problems, or other life stresses. In psychiatric terms, these are known as adjustment disorders. After a short time, these moods usually lift, and the person will function normally again.

The diagnostic definition for a major depression is a depressed mood for most of each day, which lasts more than two months. Symptoms may include:

1. Poor appetite or overeating
2. Insomnia or hypersomnia (inability to sleep)
3. Low energy or fatigue
4. Either a slowing down or a speeding up of one's activities and mental processes, nearly every day
5. Diminished interest in pleasurable activities
6. Low self esteem

7. Significant weight gain or loss when not dieting
8. Poor concentration or difficulty in making decisions
9. Feelings of hopelessness, and experiencing thoughts of death or suicide

To qualify as a major depressive disorder, at least five of the above symptoms must be present over a two-week period.

Depression can masquerade as different ailments—headache, ulcers, fatigue and anxiety—and can often be dismissed as "the blues." The blues often leave in a few days, but a full-blown depression can last up to six months or more.

Different Forms of Depression

There are different forms of depression. *Melancholic Depression* is a condition in which the individual has lost interest or pleasure in all activities and doesn't improve even when something good happens. Most people with a major depressive disorder are able to be cheered up at least temporarily.

Dysthymia is a mild depression. The term means "ill-humored." People with dysthymia never feel really well. To be classified as dysthymia the condition must have been present at least two years.

Manic-Depressive Disorder is a bipolar disorder because it involves alternating episodes of serious mania and depression. There is much variation in the disorder, but they are differentiated by highs and lows and periods in between. Some people have repeated depressions and only occasional episodes of mania, while others have "mixed mood disorder" in which they experience intense depression and mania at the same time. A very small group of people experience only manic episodes.

A person in a manic phase will have some or all of these symptoms: (1) decreased need for sleep, (2) increased energy, (3) unrealistic beliefs in his own abilities and powers, (4) increased risk-taking, (5) extreme euphoria, distractibility, and irritability, (6) obnoxious, provocative, or intrusive behavior, (7) increased talking and physical, social and sexual activity, and (8) abuse of drugs, alcohol and sleeping medications.

Many Causes of Depression

There are many causes of depression, but the precise way that depression occurs has not yet been fully discovered and defined. *Biochemical and psychosocial factors* can both contribute to depression, which begins with a disturbance in the brain that governs moods. Both depression and mania have been associated with improper functioning of neurotransmitters, which are the chemical messengers in the brain that transmit electrical signals from one nerve cell to another. A deficit of neurotransmitters (norepinephrine, serotonin, and dopamine) can cause depression, irritability, and impulsive behavior, whereas an excess of neurotransmitters may cause mania.

People with depressive disorder may also have *endocrine disorders*. The endocrine system is the network of glands that release hormones into the bloodstream. Hyperthyroidism (increased thyroid function) can cause symptoms similar to mania, while hypothyroidism (reduced thyroid function) can cause depression. Symptoms can be alleviated by correcting the hormonal imbalance.

Most people can handle everyday stress because their bodies adjust to the pressures. However, when the stress is too great for a person, cortisol (a steroid hormone that is secreted during prolonged stress) builds up and can trigger depression. In studies with patients who were unipolar or bipolar, researchers found that about half had elevated levels of cortisol in their blood or urine that returned to normal when patients recovered from their depression.

Other Illnesses with Depression Symptoms

Some illnesses may produce the same symptoms as depression, such as mononucleosis, Epstein-Barr disease, chronic fatigue syndrome, head injury, diabetes, and kidney or liver dysfunction, Dialysis patients are especially susceptible. In addition, neurological conditions, such as stroke and Parkinson's disease; cardiovascular disease; and deficiency of some vitamins and minerals (particularly vitamins B6, B12, and folate) can produce symptoms.

Medication-induced Depression

Some medications can induce depression. Included are cardiovascular drugs, such as digitalis; psychotropics, such as benzodiazepine; some substances used to treat infection, inflammation or cancer; hormonal supplements, such as oral contraceptives (because of their progesterone content); and anabolic steroids.

Depression Caused by Life Events

No one knows for sure what triggers depression, but researchers have come to believe that 86 percent of major depressions were precipitated by a real-life event.

In my case, there were many factors. Nutritional deficiency, death of a loved one, a perceived lack of support from others, hormonal changes after birth, postpartum depression, loss, grief, guilt, anger, excessive and prolonged stress as I hopelessly watched my husband die, and feeling trapped—all these feelings and situations were involved. Now, I know that I could have helped alleviate my depression much faster with adequate nutrients and supplements, exercise, support groups, homeopathy, yoga, meditation, and an alternative practitioner.

Don't Make Depression a Permanent Guest

Despicable depression knocks at every door, but you don't have to invite it in as a permanent guest. Like my grandfather used to say, "Fresh fish and house guests shouldn't stay more than three days." If depression or the "blues" stays more than a few weeks, someone needs to move.

Picture yourself reaching out and touching the hem of the garment of Christ and feeling virtue and healing flow unto you.

Your assignments for this chapter:
1. Gratitude:
   - Write five things or people you are thankful for.
   - Thank God for helping you to be joyous in this day.
2. Read and memorize these affirmations six times a day:
   - Happiness flows through me like a river of love.
   - My mood is elevated and happy.

4
Using Nutritional Supplements and Foods to Fight Depression

*Whatsoever was the father of a disease,
an ill diet was the mother.*

—Chinese proverb

Eating Affects our Moods and Feelings

What we eat directly influences how we feel. Depression, mood swings, anxiety, fatigue, memory loss, sleep, and anger all can be traced to the foods we eat. A new car is such a fine-tuned instrument that you would never pour cola into the gas tank or put fruit punch into the oil spout. This would gum up the engine and the car wouldn't run. The body and the brain are so much more complicated and intricate than any piece of machinery, but we are constantly shoveling junk food, saturated fatty acids, and toxins into our mouths.

Neurons and Neurotransmitters

You have the power to change and enhance your own body chemistry. Everything you do is influenced by billions of nerve cells in your brain, called neurons. In order to communicate you need neurotransmitters (the chemical language of the brain) to connect the messages or trigger the neurons. Your body has about 100 billion neurons. The neurotransmitters dopamine, serotonin, and norepinephrine are controlled by what you eat or what is absorbed by your body. Dopamine and norepinephrine are the master energizers, while serotonin is the great calmer. All are in competition with one another.

Amino Acids Regulate Behavior

Amino acids form the neurotransmitters that transmit information and regulate our behavior. An imbalance of amino acids can trigger depression or mood swings. Your body uses amino acids and enzymes to break down food into basic nutrients, which are absorbed by villi in your small intestine. If you were to take the water and fat out of the body, amino acids would make up 75 percent of what remains.

Eating carbohydrates alone (without protein) will increase serotonin and may have a calming effect, while consuming proteins will increase dopamine, and norepinephrine; thereby increasing alertness and energy.

When eating proteins, choose foods such as turkey or salmon which are high in tryptophan and low in saturated fats. Tryptophan is the amino acid that processes serotonin.

Fats inhibit the synthesis of neurotransmitters by the brain because they cause the blood cells to become sticky and clump together, resulting in poor circulation, especially to the brain.

Everything from the neurotransmitters to the protein your body uses to run and rebuild itself are created from singular, isolated amino acids. Amino acids are the chemical units that make up protein. In order to be a complete protein, it must contain all of its particular amino acids.

The central nervous system cannot function without amino acids. Unless all of the amino acids are present, anything can go wrong with the transmission of the message. The liver produces about 80 percent of the amino acids we need, but the remaining essential amino acids must be obtained from our diet. Essential amino acids include arginine, histidine, isoleucine, leucine, lysine, methionine, phenylalanine, threonine, tryptophan, and valine.

If the diet is improperly balanced and there is a deficiency of essential amino acids, physical and emotional disorders will arise. In order to avoid problems, eat a balanced diet or take supplements containing essential amino acids. Vitamins and minerals will not be effective unless amino acids are present.

Tyrosine is an amino acid needed for brain function. It serves as the starting point in the manufacture of several important neurotransmitters. Studies of depressed people have shown that many have low levels of tyrosine in the brain. According to Dr. Julian Whitaker, founder of the Whitaker Wellness Institute in Newport Beach, California, "Supplementing the diet with L-tyrosine has been shown to be as effective as antidepressant drugs without the side effects. Start out by taking 2,000 milligrams, three times per day before meals. After one month, drop the dosage by half."

This information is meant to inform and educate you, not to replace medical advice. It would be a good idea to discuss L-tyrosine and other amino acids with a health practitioner before trying Dr. Whitaker's recommended dosage. Tyrosine should not be taken with MAO and tricyclic antidepressants or when a cancerous melanoma is present.

Prescription Antidepressants

If you are taking any prescription antidepressant or other drugs for mental or anxiety disorders, do not stop taking these drugs unless you are under the care of a health practitioner. This can throw you into a terrible tailspin. If you have a medication that is working for you, then keep taking it. If not, consult your doctor. You must be weaned off most prescription antidepressants gradually. I have seen individuals become suicidal when they immediately discontinue medications.

If you are bipolar, do not substitute nutritional supplements for your medication, but you can improve your diet. The individual amino acid supplements in this chapter are options to be discussed with a health practitioner for those people who are depressed and not already taking medications. However, it is likely that most individuals can take a balanced amino acid supplement such as vegetarian protein powder.

Phenylalanine and methionine can also be used for depression. Phenylalanine helps maintain a positive mood, and alertness, as well as enhancing learning and memory. In addition, it helps suppress the appetite.

Amino acids can be purchased as powders, capsules, and tablets. Most are derived from egg protein, animal protein, or yeast protein. I prefer a protein powder made from vegetarian sources (usually soy). I usually mix this with pure organic apple juice.

Homeopathic Remedies

There are homeopathic remedies that can help people come off medications that are not working for them, but these must be discussed with an expert in homeopathy. One of the advantages of homeopathic remedies is that they do not have side effects and can be taken with most prescription medications or other nutrients.

My physician gives his patients the following list of options for depression:

1. Avoid refined sugar, alcohol, and caffeine.
2. Eat fish, pineapple, bananas, avocado, cabbage, tomatoes, and plums.
3. Engage in more physical activity
4. St. John's Wort, 300 mg., 3 times a day (it won't help bipolar disorder)
5. Take Siberian Ginseng, 200 mg., 3 times a day
6. B-12/folic acid shots (prescription) or Sublingual B drops
7. Take Magnesium 250 mg. a day.
8. Take B Complex Vitamins
9. Take Niacin, 100—500 mg., 3 times a day (start with 25 mg because niacin causes flushing)
10. Take Li-zyme Lithium, 5 mcg., a day (mainly for bipolar disorder)
11. Take Vitamin C, 2000 mg., 3 times a day
12. Take Ginkgo Biloba (an herb), 40 mg., 3 times a day
13. Take L-tryptophan, 500—4000 mg. (prescription)
14. Take Johimbine (over-the-counter and prescription)

Obviously, these are not meant to be taken all together. You would not take all of the above supplements, but only nutrients essential to your own body.

Kinesiology Muscle Testing

Since no two people have the same body chemistry, everyone's nutritional needs are not the same. Your body knows it's own nutritional needs and what is best.

How do you determine what is best for you? What I'm going to discuss now is sometimes a little controversial, but something I strongly believe in and use myself—kinesiology muscle testing, Biokinesiology, or Behavioral Kinesiology (BK). Biokinesiology unites creative meditation, nutritional supplementation, and exercise for optimum health. BK is a combination of kinesiology, psychiatry, psychosomatic medicine, preventive medicine, and the humanities. Dr. John Diamond, a psychiatrist and expert in BK, and author of the book on muscle testing, *Your Body Doesn't Lie*, believes and demonstrates that you can ask your own body what is best for your health. It is based on the theory that foods or chemicals to which an individual is sensitive can cause muscle weakness as a result of changing the body's electrical field. You can test foods or individual supplements by testing the muscles to see if they are weak. Both Biokinesiology and BK use the deltoid muscle (the muscle that cap the shoulder and helps lift the arm). Tisha Mecham, in her book, *Bio-Kinetic Testing For Health*, writes about taking the guesswork out of healing and has some excellent illustrations on muscle testing. It is available at P.O. Box 313, Sandy, Ut. 84091-0313.

Before testing, the testee should think the word "*Mild.*" The testing process involves two people: the testee and the tester. The testee should stand erect and put his arm straight out, horizontally, with the palm down. The tester will place his hand on the subject's arm just above the wrist, and will have the testee resist as he pushes his arm down. He should press down gently for several seconds while the subject resists. Do this several times to test the strength of the arm. With the right amount of pressure the arm will lock in place. Now, the testee should place the nutrient under his tongue or in his opposite hand. Next, the tester should gently push the testee's arm down. If it locks in place, his body wants the nutrient; but if the muscle is weak and his arm goes down, his body does not want or need the nutrient at the present time.

Following are several of the muscle tests that I most frequently use. You will need a partner or tester for the first test. Place your thumb and "pinky" (little finger) together with the balls of the finger and thumb connected, and hold the two closed tightly. Next, while you say your name, have your partner try to gently pull the thumb and finger apart. If the pressure in pulling or separating the two sets of muscles is gentle and accurate, the finger and thumb will not separate because the muscles will test strong. You may have to experiment with this several times to get the right pressure. Now, say "My name is Karen (or Dave or any other fictitious name)," as your partner tries to separate your fingers. Again, if the pressure is accurate, the fingers will separate easily and quickly. When it is a true statement, the muscles will stay together. When false, they will separate. You may test food or nutrients by holding the supplements in the opposite hand or close to your body near the thymus (upper breastbone). If your muscles stay strong (close together), the nutrients are needed; if they separate, they are not essential right now. Sometimes I have individuals say, "You pulled harder this time." Then I recommend they try another partner and experiment with muscle testing.

A way to muscle test by yourself is to stand erect, face North, with your feet relaxed and comfortably apart, and hold the nutrient in your relaxed hands next to the thymus or solar plexus (center of the abdomen just above the navel). Relax, and just let your body guide you. Do not try to move your body; allow it to go with the flow and let your body move forward or backward as it desires. If you move forward, the nutrient is good for you; if backward, the nutrient is not what you need at the present time. I usually test with sugar first, and only once have I had an individual move forward on sugar (meaning the body can tolerate it). Sugar weakens the immune system. Most people will move forward with an apple or banana.

Occasionally I will have people whose energy is so out of balance they cannot muscle test accurately or cannot test.

Putting one's tongue at the roof of the mouth behind the front teeth for several minutes will help balance energy. Also, imagine yourself being bathed in a healing white light from head to toe. Reading poetry and deep breathing are also other options to balance energy.

Once, while I was teaching muscle testing to a small group of medical doctors who were very skeptical, one of them muscle tested a chocolate bar and leaned way back. He was astonished and said, "This works! I don't know why it works, but it works."

Chiropractors and naturopaths frequently use muscle testing and some are very knowledgeable about nutrition. While speaking about alternative medicine a physician said to me, "For fourteen years I practiced traditional medicine, but during that time I had all of these patients coming to me who were going to chiropractors and getting well. Finally I decided to look into alternative medicine, and now it's part of my practice."

Once, during an office visit, I asked an osteopathic physician if he used muscle testing. Although he believed in it, he didn't use it in his practice, but he brought into the room twenty nutritional supplements so I could muscle test myself and evaluate what my body needed at that particular time.

Hypoglycemia and Sugar Problems

Avoid refined sugar and simple carbohydrates with empty calories. The body reacts more quickly to the presence of sugar than complex carbohydrates, and an increase in energy from sugar is quickly followed by fatigue and depression. Sugar has no nutrients, and it weakens the immune system. Complex carbohydrates raise the level of tryptophan and have a calming effect. According to Dr. Larry Christensen, an expert on the effects of sugar and caffeine on mood, "Consuming too much sugar or caffeine definitely contributes to feelings of depression for sensitive individuals."

In one study conducted by Dr. Christensen, 20 people with serious depression were asked to cut sugar and caffeine from their diets. After three weeks, these individuals were significantly less depressed.

Hypoglycemia, meaning low sugar in the blood, is a condition in which the body chronically produces too much insulin. This can cause depression, weakness, fatigue, irritability, trembling, anxiety, confusion, suicidal tendencies, faintness, and palpitations. Glucose is a form of sugar your body makes from food; it provides the energy for all your cellular activities. When blood glucose and mineral stores become depleted, your body cells cannot produce adequate energy. Of all your organs, the brain is the most dependent on the continual supply of glucose from the blood, and when the blood sugar drops, the brain immediately suffers, causing fatigue and emotional chaos. Although glucose can be manufactured from proteins and fats, carbohydrates are most rapidly converted to glucose.

If you have low blood sugar, avoid junk foods, sugar, alcohol, and white bread. Eat frequent meals high in complex carbohydrates and vegetable protein. Include whole foods (raw) such as fruits, vegetables, seeds nuts, whole grains, oats, brown rice and millet. In addition, spirulina or protein powders help prevent a low blood sugar reaction.

Dr. Carl C. Pfeiffer recommends daily exercise, plus taking 10 milligrams manganese gluconate morning and evening, 15 milligrams zinc morning and evening, vitamin B3 plus chromium (GTF) morning and evening, and a daily multivitamin tablet without copper.

Glucose cannot be stored or used without vitamins, minerals, and trace elements. These include vitamin C, B complex, calcium, potassium, magnesium, zinc, chromium, manganese, and phosphorous.

B complex vitamins are essential for depression. They are known as co-enzymes and are required before food can turn into fuel. For most depressed clients, my doctor recommends a sublingual (liquid) B-complex because it is in the blood stream within a few minutes after it is consumed.

Candida Albicans and Depression

Candida albicans is a yeast-like fungus that inhabits the gastrointestinal tract, mouth, throat, genital tract, and bowels. This fungus normally lives in healthy balance with other bacteria and yeasts in our body, but some conditions, such as taking antibiotics, can cause this fungus to multiply, weakening the immune system and causing an infection known as candidiasis. Yeasts are single-cell living organisms that live on the surfaces of all living things, including grains, fruits, vegetables, and your skin. Mildew, mold, mushrooms and candida are all different types of yeast.

Antibiotics can't wipe out candida yeasts, and so they multiply and grow in the intestinal tract and other areas of our body, weakening the immune system. When you take more antibiotics, the yeast thrives, and it raises havoc with the immune system. Your body craves sugar and breads, which in turn promotes more yeast overgrowth.

Candida overgrowth can contribute to "leaky gut" syndrome. Normally in the digestion process, villi in the intestines absorb nutrients from your food into the blood stream, but with the candida overgrowth clogging the system, toxins and food allergens pass through the membrane and into other parts of your body. This makes you feel sick all over. As these candida colonies produce powerful toxins that affect your immune system, hormone balance, and thought processes, depression progresses. Vital nutrients needed for the brain are not absorbed.

Common symptoms of candida are constipation or diarrhea, abdominal bloating, anxiety, environmental sensitivities, food sensitivities, fuzzy thinking, insomnia, low blood sugar, mood swings, premenstrual syndrome, ringing in the ears, recurring bladder or vaginal infections, and sensitivities to perfume, petroleum products, cigarettes or fabric odors.

Many physicians do not recognize candida in a systemic form, but for those who do, it is a common diagnosis. Alternative health care practitioners are more likely to identify candida as an underlying health problem.

My personal physician believes that candida is the cause of eighty-five percent of the cases of Chronic Fatigue Syndrome. Dr. Abraham Hoffer, a renowned orthomolecular psychiatrist, states that one third of the world's population suffers from candidiasis.

In the 1980's Dr. Hoffer treated a patient who had suffered severe depression for many years with nystatin (a prescription for fungal problems). Within one month she was mentally and emotionally normal.

Dr. William C. Crook, author of *"The Yeast Connection,"* writes of a woman who suffered from manic depression for eight years and gained little help from traditional medicines. Her general practitioner finally prescribed a diet, nystatin and nutritional supplements. Within three months, her symptoms were gone.

Treatment for candida can involve the traditional medicines such as nystatin, or diflucan. It is important to avoid fruit, dried fruit, all sugars, flours, grains, aged cheeses, alcoholic beverages, mushrooms, vinegar or yeasted breads. Almost all commercial breads, cakes, and crackers contain yeast, so be sure to read the labels. Avoid chemical household products and cleaners, chlorinated water, mothballs, synthetic fabrics, and damp and moldy places. Remember that antibiotics, birth control pills, and hormones can cause or contribute to candidiasis.

There are nonprescription probiotics such as Lactobacillus acidophilus and Bifidium bacterium products that help limit or retard the growth of candida. Others include caprylic acid (which includes psyllium because it helps clean out fecal matter), citrus seed extract, garlic (raw or deodorized in capsules), tanalbit, Pau D' Arco tea, and goldenseal. Goldenseal can lower blood sugar.

Do eat brown rice, brown rice cakes, millet, oats, buckwheat, vegetables and bananas. Other good choices are avocados, asparagus, beets and greens, broccoli, carrots, cauliflower, celery, cucumbers, endive, garlic, lettuce, onions, parsley, parsnips, peas, soybeans, spinach, fresh tomatoes, turnips, and potatoes. Salmon, tuna and white fish are the most healthful choices of meat, but you can eat chicken, turkey, lean beef, veal, lamb, and wild game. All breads, biscuits and muffins should be made with baking powder or baking soda instead of yeast. Unsweetened applesauce should be used instead of sugar.

Types of Depression and their Nutritional Relationships

Dr. Carl C. Pfeiffer, an expert in orthomolecular psychiatry, has written an excellent book, *Nutrition and Mental Illness*. Throughout his life he has done extensive research into nutrition and mental illness and treated more than 25,000 patients successfully. He maintains there are five biotypes of schizophrenias: (1) *Histapenia*—due to low blood histamine with excess copper (50 percent of the schizophrenias), (2) *Histadelia*—high blood histamine with low copper (20 percent), (3) *Pyroluria*—a familial double deficiency of zinc and vitamin B6 (30 percent) (4) *Cerebral allergy*—includes wheat-gluten allergy (10 percent) and (5) *Nutritional hypoglycemia*—(20 percent of schizophrenias).

In his book, he lists specific supplements that have successfully helped these biotypes and individual patients. Regarding manic-depressive illness, Dr. Pfeiffer states, "Most of the patients who come to the Brain Bio Center [his clinic in New Jersey] with a diagnosis of manic-depressive illness and have weekly swings in mood are merely pylouric. They are easily treated with adequate zinc and B6."

My advice is to do your own research and check with a competent health-care professional.

In his book, *Natural Prozac*, Dr. Joel Robertson, a doctor of pharmacology, discusses two types of personalities that are depressed. The first is *Satiation Depression*, characterized by lethargy, confusion, withdrawal, and an inability to concentrate. He recommends raising your serotonin, and gently raising your norepinephrine and dopamine to give you a greater sense of personal power and control in your life. He also recommends foods that will boost serotonin. L-tyrosine also boosts serotonin.

The second type of personality is the *Arousal-Depressed Personality* who has extremely low serotonin levels coupled by relatively high to extremely high levels of norepinephrine and dopamine. These people are always in motion, action oriented, and always on the go. Among other feelings, they feel anxious, pressured, tense, stressed, afraid, tired, and overworked. They are like the "stick that is always stirring things up." Dr. Robertson says, the strategy here is ". . . to raise your serotonin and gently lower norepinephrine and dopamine." He recommends eliminating protein-rich foods, caffeine, refined carbohydrates such as sugar, white flour, all alcohol, and replacing them with whole grains, fresh vegetables, and beans.

For more information on orthomolecular medicine, contact Dr. Richard Kunin, 2968 Pacific Avenue, San Francisco, California, 94115, or call 415-922-6462.

Your assignments for this chapter:
1. Memorize the following affirmations:
   - The universe feeds my soul with harmonious experiences.
   - My body, soul and spirit are well nourished.
   - I easily digest and assimilate my food.
   - Each cell in my body is replenished and energized.
   - My neurotransmitters work in perfect harmony.

2. Express your gratitude in prayer:
   Thanks, God, (or Higher Power) for helping me find the right supplements and nutrition that my body needs to be healthy.

5
Instantaneous Activities that Help Fight Depression

Trust in the Lord with all thy heart; and lean not unto thine own understanding. In all thy ways acknowledge him, and he shall direct thy paths.

—Proverbs 3:5-6

Life is full of mountains and valleys, and most crises do pass. But until they do, how do you hold yourself together?

The following suggestions will give you something to hang on to when you feel you have nothing left:

- Are you doing things you love to do, or are you living your life for someone else?
- Remember, these feelings will pass.
- Talk to someone, either on the phone or in person.
- Resolve to live one more day. You probably won't feel much worse tomorrow than you do now, and you may feel a lot better.
- It's always darkest before the dawn.
- Try to "sleep on it." Things always look better in the daylight.
- Go about your normal activities. Staying in the mainstream of life keeps your mind busy.
- If you can't sleep, a health food store should have natural remedies. Try counting backwards from one hundred.
- Keep saying the following affirmation: "*A kind and forgiving world sings me to a peaceful sleep.*"
- Take a deep breath clear down to your navel and blow it out your mouth. Repeat and silently say "peaceful sleep," as you breathe

in, and "stress" as you blow out. Breathe in "peaceful sleep," blow out "stress." Repeat over and over until you feel relaxed and ready to sleep. It normally takes fifteen minutes to fall asleep once your head hits the pillow. If you fall asleep immediately, you may be suffering from exhaustion.
- Dance to the rhythm of some lively music. Once I had a small group of teenagers in my office who were all feeling depressed. I turned on some jazzy music, had them dance and snap their fingers to the beat of the music and within a few minutes they were all laughing. Some of them were laughing at each other, but it didn't matter, they felt better.
- Meditate.
- Don't withdraw from others. Be with people at least for brief periods of time. Someone who has suffered depression or the blues might be easier to talk with because they understand your pain.
- Keep busy.
- Control your thoughts. When your mind is not occupied you tend to dwell on negative thoughts. Check your thoughts for three minutes. Write down a "P" for positive thoughts and an "N" for negative thoughts. Now add up all the positives and negatives. Are you a positive or negative thinker? You can control your thoughts, but you have to work on it. If you're playing negative tapes in you head, replace the thoughts with positive tapes. You create your own head music. (A later chapter will deal with positive affirmations.)
- Depression makes you feel worthless, hopeless, and useless. Recognize that these feelings are the depression talking, and that they do not really represent the way life is or who you are.
- Consider your domain of influence for good versus your problems or worries. Put aside that worry and for right now do what you do well, or plan something fun.
- Think back to when you were a small child and find that inner child that used to laugh, love, and play. What was your favorite game as a child? What made you laugh? Depressed persons have frequently lost that inner child and are very serious adults.

- Pray.
- No one really wants to die—they just don't know how to go on living right now.
- Psychologists tell us that sharing our feelings with others helps protect us from extreme mental stress, so find someone to talk to. Forrest Gump talked to strangers. "My mother always said that life is like a box of chocolates. You never know what you are going to get." To him, everyone was a potential friend.
- If we lock ourselves in a jail of self-pity, we are the jailers who hold the keys.
- My grandmother used to say, "Don't let your pity party last more than two minutes."
- Attitude is the mind's paint brush. It can color any situation.
- There is nothing in this life that cannot be fixed.
- Unhappiness and sorrow are not forever.
- What is the best thing you've ever done for yourself? What is the best activity you can do now?
- Take a nature walk. Ralph Waldo Emerson wrote, "Though we travel the world over to find the beautiful, we must carry it with us or we will not find it."
- If you always do what you've always done, you'll always get what you always got.
- Focus on your successes in life and record or write them down.
- Two people can do anything as long as one of them is your higher power.
- Visualize yourself talking to your hero or someone whom you admire or respect. Imagine them embracing you with love and caring.
- Remember, there are thousands of options in life. Search for all possible solutions. Brainstorm and write them down right now, even if they seem off the wall.
- If you were a stand-up comic, what would you say about your situation? Try this in front of a mirror.
- Regenerate by taking a trip to a tropical island, fishing, or somewhere you can afford to go.

- Get away for a few days. Walk on the beach, visit a lake or stream. Have fun. Take time to heal!
- If you don't take care of yourself no one else will.
- Hit a pillow.
- Each new day is the beginning of the rest of your life.
- Make a new beginning. It's hard to be depressed if you have long-range goals that you are passionately seeking.
- Laughter is a tranquilizer with no side affects. Laugh, laugh, laugh.
- Mentally reach out and take hold of the hem of the garment of Christ and feel virtue (healing) flow unto you.
- Someone out there needs you. You may be the answer to their prayers. Volunteer at a charitable agency.
- Go to the park and feed the ducks.
- Hum, sing or chant.

In his book, *Music Miracles*, Don Campbell explains there are sounds that deplete human energy, and other sounds that bring strength and vitality. "Drumming, harmonious singing, chanting, lyric harp playing and rapturous organ music all create altered states of perception and evoke awakenings."

While living in Japan, Campbell, who is a musician, teacher, and trainer, was having life-threatening asthmatic attacks and was sent to a Manchurian doctor who treated allergies. The doctor simply asked him to place his palms on top of the doctor's palms for two minutes. Campbell said he experienced warm energy and electricity in his hands and his breathing quickly became deep and free. The physician told Don he could help him if he came twice a week for two months while the doctor "put the missing tones" back into his body. Each visit the doctor burned herbs in a tone lamp while Don soaked his feet in hot water for five minutes. Within two months his asthmatic attacks stopped, never to return.

Some years later, Campbell developed a degenerative bone condition and a lump in his left lung. Despondent, depressed and without much interest in even his music, he then remembered the power of transformation of sounds and tone. He began chanting. Then he said,

"I entered deeply into tone. I felt the power of one tone, one sound, so full, so complete I lost track of time." For twelve hours, all night and into the morning, he held a tone.

Campbell describes the tone, ". . . like an open mouth hum, powerfully vibrating my body, massaging me from the inside out."

He continued toning for an additional twenty-four hours while he listened to Bach's "St. Matthew's Passion," the music of Terry Riley, sacred Indian ragas and Gregorian Chant. "My body and mind became one vibrating wave, and a strange sense of completion and fullness began to emerge. No trace of the lump or the pain in my bones ever recurred."

Some of the above suggestions may make you angry. That's okay, maybe some will make you think or give you hope to go on. The important thing is to take action, because you're less likely to be depressed if you're "moving."

A story is told of a bunch of turkeys that attended a workshop to enhance their flying ability. Among other things, they were taught how to take off, to soar, and to gain momentum and altitude. After the workshop they all walked home. We are sometimes like that, we have the knowledge but are not living what we know.

Your assignments for this chapter:
1. Gratitude:
   - I am grateful for uplifting music.
   - Write down five things that you are grateful for.

2. Write down and memorize these affirmations:
   - I have all of the power I need to change my life.
   - My mind is functioning perfectly.
   - I am finding new and creative ways to live.

*Believe that life is worth living
and your belief will create the fact.*

—William James

6
Developing a Support System

*The fragrance of the rose
lingers in the hand of the giver.*

—Confucius

Easing Other's Burdens Through Support Groups

When I was first widowed I was in tremendous emotional pain and ached with loneliness. As I began to heal, I wanted to help other widows or divorcees who were experiencing what I had gone through. I started a support group for single women so that they could join and receive help at the beginning of their anguish. Not that I think we can or should carry the pain of someone else; we each have to experience our own sorrow, but we can ease the burdens of others by caring and being there. I wanted others to know that no matter what happens to you, you can go on from where you are and grow. Sometimes life's difficulties are our greatest teachers.

At our first meeting we had a book review of *With Twelve You Get Egg Roll*. Of the original twelve women who attended, all of them eventually remarried. Over the years we had more than two hundred women join our group, and the group is still meeting and inviting others to join. We were like a large extended family working together to help each other. Everyone had it tough, but no one whined. The goal was to grow spiritually and make the best of our lives.

We did all kinds of activities together. We had Sunday evening sing-alongs and served grilled cheese sandwiches. Several times we rented a chalet and took our children. There was one large room for the women and another for all the guys. We attended singles dances. We had adult parties at our homes where we played croquet, volley ball, Ping-Pong, and danced on the patio. Once a month we had potluck dinners. We shopped thrift stores and garage sales and learned about living on a strict budget.

When Holly's old car reached a hundred thousand miles, she had a birthday party for the car. At Christmas we shared white elephant gifts. I remember getting hip-waders decorated with flowers, a gunnysack bathing suit, and old-fashioned long bloomers that were size 40—way too large for any of us. Comradery and humor connected us and helped us heal.

How did I meet all of the women? Like a magnet, I was drawn to meet single women at grocery stores, at church, at school, at the doctors office, and through other friends. Somehow I could feel their pain even before I knew they were single, and a voice inside me whispered "they need a support group." Women heard about our group and wanted to join, and when they did they usually had a friend or relative who also wanted to meet with us.

There are all kinds of support groups available in most communities. If you can't find the one you're looking for in the phone book, check your local library for "self-help support groups." Also, check the Internet. If you don't have access to the Internet, most libraries have it.

One of my favorite support groups is Alanon or any twelve-step program. Groups are free and the twelve-step approach is a wonderful process for healing.

The support we receive from family, friends, and professionals during times of stress and depression plays an important role in our reaction to our difficulties. The opportunity to love and be loved, and to share joy or pain, is one of the great gifts of life. Interactions we have with supportive people help us feel better faster.

Five Categories of Helping Behavior

Now, grab a piece of paper because I want you to identify your support network. In the first column write the name of the people you would go to for support. Check if the individual is a professional, which would include doctors and counselors, or a family member, co-worker, roommate, club or association member, religious leader, partner, spouse, family member, or support group.

Name	Spouse	Partner	Family	Friend	Co-worker	Professional	Religious leader	Support Group	Kind of Support

Support from people during stressful events or depression can be broken down into five categories of helping behaviors. First: *Emotional Support*—someone listening to your private thoughts and feelings or giving you physical affection; Second: *Material Aid Support*—someone lending you money or the use of a valuable object, like a car or appliance during times of great stress; Third: *Advice and Information*—someone suggesting what to do or where to get needed help or information; Fourth: *Physical Assistance*—someone helping you with jobs around the house, errands or favors you might need during stress; and Fifth: *Social Participation*—someone offering you the opportunity to engage in pleasant social activities.

Now go through your entire support list. What kind of support does each person give you? Is this reciprocal? Can each person on your list come to you for support during times of stress? Are you happy with your support system? Do you need to add to your support system? Do you have a friend or support group that can help you brainstorm on how to add to your support?

Your Spiritual Support System

Have you included your Higher Power as the mainstay of your support system? What kind of spiritual support system do you have?

I believe everyone has a guardian angel. Articles about guardian angels are popping up all throughout the media. Several years ago my present husband had a kidney removed because of kidney cancer. He then had to go on dialysis, and while still in the hospital, suffered a heart attack. He had coronary artery disease and congestive heart failure. Shortly after, I was walking down a long hall in a place that was very sacred to me, feeling very alone. It was peaceful and serene. Suddenly I heard an inner, distinct voice say to me, "I am with you." Startled, I looked around to see if anyone was with me. As I had thought, I was all alone. Satisfied, I continued walking when I heard the voice say again, "I am with you."

"Who? Who is with me?" I asked. "Your guardian angel," the voice responded. Like a soft cloud enveloping me, I felt a warm engulfing love, but saw no one, yet felt the truth of the prompting.

In his book, *An Inquiry Into The Existence Of Guardian Angels*, Pierre Jovanovic shares a story from the *Relief Society Magazine*, August 1920, of a testimony of Peter Johnson. Johnson, hospitalized with yellow fever, found himself standing above his body and realized his spirit had left his body. He later wrote,

> ... I perceived that I was the same in the spirit as I was in the body. While contemplating the new condition, something attracted my atten-

tion, and on turning around I beheld a personage who said to me, "You did not know that I was here."

I replied: "No, but I see you are. Who are you?"

"I am your guardian angel; I have been following you constantly while on earth."

Just recently my son was in a serious motorcycle accident. He was driving 45 miles-per-hour when a car quickly pulled in front of him. There was no way to stop. The collision totaled both the car and the motorcycle, and my son was thrown twenty feet in the air. He said that several seconds before the impact, he blacked out and didn't wake up until he was on the ground. Witnesses said he landed on his head. Fortunately, he was wearing a helmet. Neither the paramedics nor the police could believe he was alive. Several times they came into the emergency room at the hospital to tell us that it was a miracle. "He should have been dead," they repeated.

He soon fell asleep from the pain medication they had given him. Alone in the x-ray room with my son, I marveled that he had survived. As I reflected upon this miracle, I suddenly felt a presence in the room—the presence of his guardian angel, who I somehow knew was a male. The impression was communicated to me that my son's life literally had been preserved by this angelic being.

The African Shaman believes that relatives that have passed on are now trying to help and impart wisdom to loved ones they left behind on earth.

Once, while alone in my bedroom, heavy-hearted from struggling with a crisis in my life, I heard my first husband say to me, "It's okay, Pat. I'm doing everything I can here to help you there."

God May Have a Better Plan than We Have

In a grocery store, I watched a father run to his weeping two-year-old daughter who had been lost in the store for a few minutes. As he swept her into his big arms, she nestled her neck upon his shoulder while he caressed her. Quickly, her frantic sobbing was quieted. My thoughts rushed to the Savior's words in Luke 13:34, ". . .how often would I have gathered thy children together, as a hen doth gather her brood under her wings, and ye would not!" How often would he gather us to his bosom, but we will not be gathered nor comforted.

My daughter went through a tragic divorce that she did not want, but ultimately it led her to God and peace in her life. While she was running around trying to "fix" everything, a wise counselor said to her, "Sometimes we need to realize that God has a better plan for us than we have for ourselves."

Remember the Lord's promise to us, "Behold I stand at the door, and knock: if any man hear my voice, and open the door, I will come in to him, and will sup with him, and he with me." (Revelation 3:20)

How often do we stand, lonely and aching, but with our tough armor shielding the door to our heart?

Your assignments for this chapter:

1. Find a support group or group of friends that you can meet with this week.

2. Write in your gratitude journal concerning your beliefs about the following:
   - I am thankful for family and friends who support me.
   - I am grateful for the Higher power that guides my life.
   - I am thankful for guardian angels who watch over me.

3. Write three or more things you are thankful for today.

4. Record and memorize some of the following affirmations:
   - Today my Higher power is directing my life, and I have learned how to meet new friends.
   - All things and people who are part of the divine plan of my creation now come into my life.
   - I am in touch with my Higher Power and He is guiding my life.
   - I am guided by a higher power to help other people.
   - I enjoy a fabulous support system.
   - I feel loved and appreciated by all that know me.

7
Utilize the Power of Positive Self-talk and Affirmations

*Keep your face to the sunshine
and you cannot see the shadows.*

—Helen Keller

Our Thoughts Determine Our Feelings and Actions

How we think determines how we feel, and how we feel often determines our actions. By developing positive self-talk, we can conquer our negative feelings. By now you've noticed the affirmations at the end of each chapter; memorize them, or record them on a cassette tape. The affirmations are to help re-program your negative, "stinking-thinking" patterns.

Dr. Ted Morter quotes Proverbs 23:7, "As a man thinketh in his heart, so is he." Morter claims we go around pleading or bargaining with God to help us, but instead we should thank Him ahead of time for the blessings we want to come into our lives. "Thanks, God, for making me healthy. Thanks for helping me know joy and peace in my life."

Negative thoughts separate us from God, and from His love. God is love.

What We think About Actually Comes into Our Life

When an African shaman prays for rain, he prays, "Thanks for the taste of the rain. Thanks for the smell of the rain. Thanks for the rain."

In reality he knows that somewhere it is raining. He's just telling the truth before it happens, and soon it starts to rain.

Dr. Wayne Dyer, a well-known psychologist, says that what we think about actually comes into our life. If we think negative thoughts, negative results will come into our life. If we think positive thoughts, positive results will come into our life. "When you realize that what you think about becomes your reality, you become very careful about what you think about," according to Dyer.

A Technique for Shoving Negative Thoughts Aside

Picture your mind as being a small train station in a quaint mountain village; as one train pulls into the station another train prepares to leave the terminal. Monitor your thoughts for two minutes, and as negative thoughts come into your mind, quickly load them onto the out-bound train. Get rid of every negative thought. When the in-bound train comes roaring through your brain and every cell in your body, load it to overflowing with positive thoughts and vibrant energy. Stack the negative thoughts in a pile and shove them aside so the porter can load them onto the out-bound train while you persist in loading the positive thoughts and affirmations. After two minutes, stop the process and write about the experience. What were your feelings?

Your subconscious mind can help you change. It does not know the difference between the truth and a lie (or an about-to-be truth). I've watched depressed or very unhappy people walk into my office, and within ten minutes of breathing in "happiness" and blowing out gloom, their mood is elevated from a two (ten is positive, one is negative) to a five or a six. If they sing, "I feel happy, oh, so happy," it sometimes raises another step.

Take a deep breath and breathe in positive energy, then breathe out negative energy. Not too many years ago, it was believed that the mind controls the body. Now we know that every cell in our body talks to every other cell within our being.

Create Your Own Affirmations

Start creating some of your own affirmations. Be specific. Remember, your subconscious mind takes everything literally, so don't limit your imagination when making affirmations. Affirmations must be in the present tense and written in a positive tone. For example, "I enjoy perfect peace of mind and balance in my life."

If you have difficulty thinking of a good affirmation, think of how things would be if they were already the way you want them.

"I enjoy being cheerful." Act as if life is positive and you are already what you want to be.

Affirmation Samples

Following are some affirmations that I have collected over the years. You can record, read, write down or say any of these on a daily basis. They will give you some ideas as you write your own affirmations.

- I am a clear channel for positive thinking.
- It is a wonderful day.
- All things that are part of the divine plan of my creation now come into my life.
- I am in communion with my higher power.
- I have all the inner peace and tranquility I need.
- I joyfully share my abundance with others.
- I have all the money I need to succeed.
- I am a child of God, filling a divinely appointed earthly mission.
- Abundance now flows into my life.
- I enjoy being happy and healthy.
- I am a worthwhile person.
- I enjoy being a positive thinker.
- Nature is cleansing my body and mind, and I am assisting in the process.
- Healing and love flows through my body like a gentle breeze caressing my soul.
- The universe is backing me up in all my obligations and decisions.

- My mind and body are healing.
- I am peaceful and serene.
- My heart is open to joy and happiness.
- I have a sense of humor.
- I enjoy laughter.
- My blood is abundant with life's energy.
- I allow myself to experience the happiness and joys of life.
- Laughing, humor and love are all positive parts of my life.
- Prosperity now comes into my life.
- I really like myself.
- I freely forgive all people and embrace them.
- I am calm, serene, and have peace of mind.
- All my thoughts are loving and happy.
- My body and spirit are in perfect alignment.
- My positive thoughts give me strength, happiness and peace.
- My life runs smoothly at all times.
- Help and support are always available to me when I need them.
- I have all of the positive power I need to take charge of my life.
- I enjoy serenity.
- I can clearly see all of the beauty surrounding me.
- I am overcoming all obstacles.
- I am creating my own happiness; no one else can create it for me.
- I am joyfully happy.
- I have the energy, time, and wisdom to make my world a happy place.
- I fill myself with love and light with each breath I take.
- I enjoy a beautiful world.
- I am releasing all the anger and frustration in my life.
- I am now happily successful.
- My body nourishes me with love and light.
- Each day I see myself becoming more successful.
- I give myself the power and permission to be a success.

- All things are working together for health, success and love in my life.
- I am calm and have peace of mind.
- My thoughts are loving and happy.
- I freely forgive everyone who has ever offended or harmed me, beginning right now.
- I see myself as a successful person.
- I enjoy helping other people as I succeed.
- Each morning is the start of an exciting new day.
- Each day is an opportunity to assert myself and make my world a marvelous place to be.
- I am a confident and extremely capable person.
- People really respect and like me.
- I have interesting, worthwhile and challenging goals.
- I am a success.
- My energy runs as clear as a mountain spring.
- My heart is open to joy and happiness.
- Each day I start fresh, at peace with the world, and at peace with myself.
- I love other people.
- I now forgive all people who need forgiving.
- I am an interesting, energetic, emphatic person who is respected and admired.
- Each day is a wonderful opportunity to begin anew.
- Each morning is the start of a new day, a fresh new look at the world.
- I free myself of all blocked energy.

If you sing affirmations three times they will usually stay in your memory. You may want to make a cassette tape of your own affirmations to play back when you need inspiration.

Oprah Winfrey did a series of television segments on positive thinking. One guest who had lived in poverty just seven years earlier had totally turned her life around by thinking positive.

She made statements over and over again affirming positives. Every negative statement or feeling she had was turned into a positive affirmation. For example, "Yesterday, I had a problem with loneliness (or money, love, with my car, my child, my job, my health, etc.). Today, my Higher Power is directing my life, and I have learned how to earn more money (find the right job, have peace in my life, etc.,)."

Your assignments for this chapter:
1. Gratitude:
   - Write or say, *Thanks for all the positive energy in my life.*
2. Write down five things that you are grateful for each day.

3. Affirmations:
   - I radiate positive friendly feelings to everyone I meet.
   - I am healthy and happy.
   - I choose thoughts that are positive, loving and empowering.
   - My life constantly changes for the better.

4. Make a tape or write down affirmations you can listen to each day.

5. Using your imagination, practice piling negative feelings on the out-bound train and positive feelings on the in-bound train for three minutes, three times a day.

8
Conquering Anger

*A soft answer turneth away wrath:
but grievous words stir up anger.*

—Proverbs 15:1

Anger Can Cause Depression and Inner Turmoil

"Anybody can become angry—that is easy; but to be angry with the right person, and to the right degree, and at the right time, and for the right purpose, and in the right way—that is not within everybody's power and is not easy," wrote Aristotle, more than two-thousand years ago.

Four things you should know about anger:
1. Anger is always a mask for other feelings.
2. Nice people get angry.
3. The events of this world don't make you angry. It is your perception of the events that trigger the anger.
4. Most of the time your anger will not help you.

Anger that we turn in on ourselves can cause depression, suicidal feelings, and an inability to perform positive action. Understanding and dealing with anger appropriately can help dissipate the depression.

Cold Anger

Cold anger is the self-destructive anger you store within you because the feelings are so difficult to express. People with cold anger feel betrayed, abandoned, rejected, helpless, let down, empty, lonely, inadequate, alone, and isolated, in addition to other negative feelings.

I am deeply concerned about this kind of anger for my clients who are seriously depressed. This is because I know that if these feelings are not properly dealt with, their depression increases, and their anger eats away at them. Cold anger shows up in other physical symptoms such as headaches, ulcers, and drug and alcohol abuse.

Suppressing Anger

Anger is a mask for other feelings including pain, hurt, and loss. When I see an angry teenager in my office, it's usually because he or she is hurting or feeling some type of loss—loss of love, loss of self-esteem, or loss of control in his life.

Stuffing our feelings, especially anger, isn't always healthy, and it's been said that feelings buried alive never die. When we choose to suppress anger, we can become depressed. Some studies have shown that people with feelings of low self-esteem, eating disorders, obesity, alcohol or drug addiction, have a marked inability to work out their anger.

Dr. William Glasser, in his book *Choice Theory*, states that when someone in our quality world is doing something we don't approve of, we become angry. If we can allow other people to conduct their lives without our need to control them, and grant others their free agency, our anger will diminish. When anger is diminished, you have less need to be depressed.

By the same token, dependency breeds hostility. When people are dependent upon us and we don't fulfill all of their needs, they become angry. They may say," I failed because you weren't there to help me," or "Where were you when I needed you?" The way to empower other people is to help them solve their own problems. Ask questions like, "What do you think is the answer? How are you going to handle the situation?"

Janet is an example of suppressing anger. She was struggling financially, so she resented the gifts of money her husband gave to his children. Because she wanted to have a good relationship with the children, she never objected. One evening as they were taking the children out to dinner for their birthday, one of his children asked to go to a little more expensive restaurant than she had anticipated. It wasn't a big deal, the cost was only about fifteen dollars more, but Janet blew her stack and made a big fuss. Everyone was in shock to see this normally kind, rational woman making such a big deal out of little matter. She felt embarrassed and totally at a loss about her behavior. The problem was that for years Janet had stuffed her feelings about bigger issues and suddenly, her feelings erupted like a tea pot ready to boil over. If she had expressed her discomfort or concerns as they happened the predicament probably wouldn't have developed.

Even Nice People Feel Anger

Nice people get angry. During my own therapy for depression, I discovered I was angry with God and with Ray—God for allowing my husband to die; Ray for abandoning me. The feelings made me feel deep guilt, which just added to my depression. At the time, my therapist pointed out that Jesus had been angry—he'd taken a whip and chased the moneychangers out of the temple. At first during my depression I didn't even know I was angry. I displaced my anger, I was angry at the world because I felt so powerless about my loss, but I couldn't talk about it. Imagine walking up to a relative and saying, "I'm furious at Ray because he died. I'm angry with God because he allowed Ray to die." Looking back now, I realize that my anger was a mask for loss, a loss of love, loss of control in my life, and a loss of self-esteem.

A furious young man uttering obscenities was ushered into my office by an uptight teacher. After the teacher left, he continued shouting obscenities and rambled on about hating the teacher, the school, and basically everything in the world. Finally, I quietly said to him, "You're really hurting, aren't you?"

He started to cry and eventually told me about the recent death of his grandfather. Here was a fatherless young man who had an unhappy relationship with his mother, and now the rock of his support system had been snatched from him in death. His fishing friend and life-long buddy and companion was gone forever. That's a lot of pain and loss for a teenager.

Classifying Your Provocations

If you can talk about your anger with a trusted friend or therapist, do so. If not, write about your angry feelings. If you're depressed and don't know what you're angry about, sit quietly for five minutes, shut your eyes and ask yourself, "What is the source of my anger? What is causing me pain?" Try to focus on the questions and listen to the answers. When you have finished, write down the thoughts or feelings that ran through your mind.

Try to understand what ticks you off—what provokes you. Four categories of aggravations include unfairness, irritations and annoyances, abuse, and frustrations. Classifying your provocations into one of the four categories will assist you in exploring your reactions. For example, if you are angry because you didn't get a raise, is that a frustration, unfairness, or abuse? Anger caused by frustration is quite different from that caused by abuse. What angers you may not ruffle someone else. Is the thing that angers you a cognitive distortion?

I once had a client we'll call Kelly, who at her employer's request, came into her office very early one morning, which set off the burglar alarm. Within ten minutes Kelly was handcuffed and found herself sitting in a police car being questioned. Furious, Kelly insisted that her boss had deliberately set up the burglar alarm so that it would go off when she put her key in the door. For several months she carried around so much cold anger that her work suffered and she was in jeopardy of losing her job. When she finally talked to her boss about the humiliation of being handcuffed and grilled by the police, she realized she was wrong about her boss. He had nothing to do with resetting the burglar alarm; a custodian had changed it without the boss's knowledge, but her "stinking thinking" had nearly cost Kelly her career.

Warm Anger

Warm anger is appropriate anger. It is the expression of your feelings before they become "hot" or "cold." Expressing warm anger lets others know what bothers you before your feelings become stuffed inside of you (cold anger), and before your anger becomes sizzling and ready to explode.

Grab a piece of paper and divide it into three columns. At the top of the page, in the first column, write "cold anger," in the second column write "warm anger," and in the third column, write, "hot anger." On the left-hand side, number your anger thermometer from the bottom up from one to ten.

	Cold Anger	Warm Anger	Hot Anger
10.			
9.			
8.			

↓ etc. down to 1

For the next week, monitor your anger. Number "one" indicates low anger and number "ten" indicates high anger. Write down in the column what caused your anger, or what you allowed to make you angry.

Expressing anger about our hurts, without using violence or temper tantrums, can help emotional wounds to heal. Some people feel it's wrong to be angry, while others feel justified at exploding at the slightest provocation. Still others seek revenge for real or imagined hurt. If everyone lived an eye-for-an-eye mentality, we'd have a lot of blind, toothless people in our world.

It used to be considered healthy to express anger; however, recent research suggests that *all* anger, expressed or suppressed, is harmful to your health and damaging to your relationships with others. Logic walks out the door when you're angry. You're likely to say things you don't mean and wouldn't say if you were rational.

How many couples have started out with a small argument that escalated as they hurled angry and insulting words at each other that were so painful they end up in a divorce?

When you're angry there is a greater risk for heart attack, stroke or hypertension. Sometimes expressed anger causes more physical damage than unexpressed anger, but what do you do with the pain that's causing your depression?

Events or people do not make us angry; it is our perception of what is happening that makes us angry. Ted's teen-age daughter was furious with him because she was grounded. "You make me so angry!" she yelled at her father. She was stamping her feet and having a tantrum when suddenly the phone rang. Totally in control, and in her sweetest voice, she answered the telephone and began a pleasant conversation with her friend. Even in the midst of a tantrum, she could control her rage.

Don't let your past control your future. Mike's first wife had been unfaithful, so when his second wife even talked to another man, he became jealous and angry. He was projecting his first wife's failings onto his present wife, even though she was totally trustworthy.

When you gauge an event or person as a threat to one of your basic needs, such as self-esteem, recognition, achievement, or social affiliation, you may be misinterpreting a provocation as a threat. When you think someone is angry with you, ask.

Most of the time, your anger will not help you. Controlling your anger does not mean denying or suppressing your feelings.

You have the choice to vent your anger openly, but what will the consequences be? Will it inflame the anger, make you feel like an idiot for losing your temper, or alienate others—especially those you love?

Techniques for Releasing Your Anger

What you can do before anger traps you:

First, take a break when you feel your anger getting hot. "I'm starting to feel angry and I'm going to take a break (or a walk or a time out)." "I'll get back to you later, after I've had time to think things through."

Return when your anger has cooled down. If it's really hot anger, it may take an hour. If you're at work, at a party, a restaurant or another place where you can't take off for an hour, go into the bathroom. You might even try pulling funny faces at yourself in the mirror. Try singing, "I feel happy. . ."

Because irritation can quickly become anger, take a time-out when you are becoming irritated. Go back to the small train station in your mind and start loading the out-bound train with negative thoughts and emotions. Put your hands on your belly and practice a belly laugh.

Second, release your anger. One technique for replacing anger is called applied kinesiology. Place your hands over the top of your breastbone in an "x" position just below your throat. This action is like pushing a button on a computer, but in this case the computer is your brain. By touching your body you are in a sense saying, "Okay brain, believe what I say." Now repeat the following words: "I now release all anger, pain and hurt, and give it to my higher power (or nature, the sea, the whales), and replace it with peace, forgiveness, love, positive energy and healing."

Repeat this activity as many times a day as needed. The words can be replaced to accommodate your needs. For example: "I now release all fear, guilt, and anxiety and give it to my higher power and replace it with serenity, self-love, calmness, and feeling connected to my higher self."

Third, use breathing exercises. Take a deep breath, and while doing so, repeat the word "peace," and then blow out "anger." Breathe in "peace," exhale "anger." Repeat this until you feel calm. Breathing deeply while repeating positive words can reprogram every cell in your body.

Fourth, use physical exertion. Walk the dog, jog, scrub the floor, do yard work, or take a brisk walk to release your anger and pent-up energy.

Your assignments for this chapter:
1. Realize when you are angry and what ticks you off. Is your anger in response to loss? What kind of loss?
2. Evaluate your thinking. Is your anger justified? Will your anger help you? What have you learned from your anger?
3. Write or talk about your anger.
4. Monitor your anger for a week.

5. Make a plan to deal with your anger in a more positive way.
6. Gratitude:
    - Thanks, God, for helping me control my negative emotions.
    - Thanks for helping me forgive.
    - Thanks for helping me sort out my thoughts in a positive way.

7. Memorize the following affirmations:
    - I now release all anger.
    - I now forgive all people who need forgiving.
    - I am releasing old negative feelings.
    - Positive thoughts flow through me.
    - As I forgive, peace comes into my life.

9
Overcoming Guilt

Sometimes the Lord calms the storm;
sometimes He lets the storm rage and calms His child.

Unloading the Guilt Bag of Unnecessary Cargo

A friend once came to me complaining of a tremendous backache. I offered to give her a shoulder massage, and as I did, I lifted her oversized purse off of the sofa so that I could sit beside her. It was so heavy, I was sure she was carrying gold bricks or lead pipes. Curious, I asked her what she carried in her bag that made it so heavy. Among other things, she emptied out two cans of hair spray, a hair-dryer, a curling iron, a hairbrush, a can of Spaghetti-o's, an anatomy book, and five tubes of lipstick. No wonder she had a backache. Although I had once carried a purse that was quite loaded, I couldn't start to top her cargo.

I pulled out the fanny pack that I had started using when my back begin to ache and emptied the contents—a tube of lipstick, a comb, checkbook, Kleenex, a small change purse, and a credit card. That was it. I no longer felt the back pain.

Sometimes we walk around in life carrying bulky, heavy bags full of unnecessary cargo until we're in so much pain we can hardly bear it. Our bags are bursting with anxiety, anger, guilt, and fear.

Healthy or Unhealthy Guilt?

We all feel guilt or shame at some time in our lives, but the question is, is it healthy or unhealthy guilt? When I was in the sixth grade I was the shortest student in the class. One day while outside for recess, I was leaning over the drinking fountain when a huge mangy dog, oblivious to my presence, quickly lifted his leg and voided at the base of the fountain, spraying my leg, my shoe, and staining my clean white anklet with yellow urine. I was humiliated, even more so when the other children gathered around me and began taunting, "Pee, pee-wee, pee-wee." Forever after, much to my shame, I was known as Pee-Wee.

Unfortunately, as an eleven-year-old, I didn't have the self-esteem to laugh at myself and joke with my peers, and every time I heard "Pee-Wee," I felt ashamed and guilty. This was not healthy guilt or shame, because I was not guilty of anything!

During a therapy session, a newly married young woman told her husband that his mother had said unkind things about her. Of course, this was a lie, but it put her mother-in-law in a bad light and negatively affected the positive relationship the mother and son had previously had. The mother-in-law was broken-hearted, and now the daughter-in-law felt guilty for her mischief. This was healthy guilt. She told her husband and apologized. Her first step was in taking responsibility for her wrong-doing, then making amends, resolving not to do it again, and then forgiving herself and moving on. She then invited her mother-in-law for dinner and patched things up with her.

All too often I see people caught in the guilt trap, literally battering and flogging themselves with negative verbal abuse on a daily basis. No wonder they are depressed. If you verbally abuse yourself, picture yourself at the other end of a firing squad, ready to be terminated. Now, peek out from beneath your blindfold and see who your executor will be. It's you! You have the power to stop firing at yourself, or you can continue your own self-abuse.

Healthy guilt means taking responsibility for our actions when we know we are wrong, seeing our mistake as an opportunity to learn, forgiving ourselves, and letting go of the pain. No matter who we are or how hard we try, we all make mistakes.

Unhealthy guilt is the kind of unwanted baggage you need to unload. When you worry about what other people think of you, or you're afraid to say "No" to others, or feel that you have to fix everything because if other people suffer or are hurt, you blame yourself for another's pain, you are experiencing unhealthy guilt. Unhealthy guilt can be toxic to your self-esteem.

Techniques for Releasing Guilt
1. Write down your unhealthy guilt feelings. Analyze them: how rational are these feelings?
2. Write down the lessons you have learned from your mistakes.
3. When you make a mistake or hurt someone, make amends the best you can. Move on and don't dwell in the past.
4. Forgive yourself for your imperfections and past mistakes.
5. Examine your good points.
6. Don't use or waste priceless energy on useless guilt.

Your assignments for this chapter:
1. Gratitude:
    - Thanks for the lessons guilt has taught me.
    - Thanks for helping me forgive myself.

2. Memorize the following affirmations:
    - I now release all guilt and move forward in my life.
    - I now forgive myself for past mistakes.
    - I am grateful that I don't have to "fix" everything.
    - I trust my Higher Power to heal me emotionally.

You gain strength, courage and confidence by every experience in which you stop and look fear in the face.

—Eleanor Roosevelt

10
Vanquishing Fear

*Of all the liars in the world, our
fears are the greatest.*

—Rudyard Kipling

The Escalating Process:
From Negative Self-talk to Worry to Fear

How we talk to ourselves determines how we feel, and we frequently run the gamut of negative self-talk. "I'm not going to pass the test." "They're not going to like me." "I can't do that."

"No one will ever love me again." Negative self-talk often leads to worry. Worry is like interest paid on a debt that never comes due. But the worst part of worry is that it sometimes escalates into fear.

I have a relative whose father died when she was four years old, and then when she was six her grandmother died. After that she had a difficult time trusting people and was afraid to get close to others. When she was in her early twenties she fell madly in love with a young man and became engaged.

After a long engagement, he broke the engagement. It was several years before she even considered dating again, but now I see her sabotaging every relationship. She sees any tiny offense, such as a date being late as an abandonment issue. She is so afraid of being hurt that she pushes everyone away.

How often in our lives do we make a bush in the dark out to be a bear?

In my office is a sign, "Worry is like a rocking chair—it gives us something to do, but it doesn't get us anywhere." Ninety-five percent of the things we worry about never happen.

Eleanor Roosevelt summed up fear, "You gain strength, courage and confidence by every experience in which you stop to look fear in the face. You are able to say to yourself, 'I lived through this horror. I can take the next thing that comes along.' You must do what you think you cannot do."

Good and Bad Fear

Three things you should know about fear:
1. Fear is an illusion.
2. Fear is your negative self-talk.
3. You can conquer fear.

Peter McWilliams, in his book, *You Can't Afford the Luxury of a Negative Thought*, agrees that we should fear some things—drinking poisons, leaping off tall buildings, and situations in which our physical body is in danger of extinction. McWilliams says, "All other fears—the ones we face most often every day—are illusions. They should be given no more credence or authority over our actions than television commercials, election-year promises, or people who try to sell us flowers in airports."

Life is sometimes like a spook-alley—the only way out is through it, but it's only temporary. It's okay to feel the fear, but then go on and do the task anyway. By doing what we fear, we can eliminate most fear in our lives.

Instead of "Awfulizing," Try "Positizing"

Our negative self-talk creates our fear. "Awfulizing" is an example: "I know something bad is going to happen." Instead of "awfulizing," try "positizing." "Thanks for helping me conquer my fear. Thanks for helping me work things out in a positive way."

One of the secrets of success is getting up when you fall down. "It matters not if you try and fail, and try and fail again; what matters most is when you try and fail, and fail to try again." Winston

Churchill's motto was "Never, never give up!" The average honey bee visits a thousand flowers to fill it's sac just once.

Fear Leads to Distrust

Fear can teach us not to trust. A teen-ager that felt abandoned because he had not seen his father in three years was sharing his feelings with me. I asked him what lessons he had learned from this experience. "I've learned that I will never leave my own children." Then he paused, "I've learned not to trust."

When I was doing drug and alcohol counseling I saw considerable mistrust and fear in my clients. The following is a handout from the substance abuse clinic where I worked.

PLEASE. . . . HEAR WHAT I'M NOT SAYING

Don't be fooled by me. Don't be fooled by the mask I wear.

For I wear a mask. I wear a thousand masks. Masks that I'm afraid to take off, and none of them is me. Pretending is an art that is second nature with me, but don't be fooled.

I give the impression that I'm secure; that all is sunny and unruffled with me, within as well as without; that confidence is my name and coolness is my game; that the waters are calm and I'm in command, and I need no one. But don't believe it, please don't.

My surface may seem smooth, but my surface is my mask; my ever varying and ever-concealing mask. Beneath dwells the real me; in confusion, in fear, in loneliness. But I hide this. I don't want anybody to know it. I panic at the thought of my weaknesses being exposed. That's why I frantically create masks to hide behind; nonchalant, sophisticated facades to help me pretend; to shield me from the glance that knows. But such a glance is precisely my salvation, my only salvation. And I know it. It's the only thing that can liberate me from myself; from my own self-built prison walls; from the barriers that I so painstakingly erect. But I don't tell you this. I don't dare. I'm afraid to.

I'm afraid your glance will not be followed by love and acceptance. I'm afraid that you will think less of me; that you'll laugh and your laugh will kill me. I'm afraid that deep down inside I'm nothing; that I'm just no good, and that you'll see and reject me. So I play my games; my desperate, pretending games, with a facade of assurance yet the trembling child within. And so begins the parade of masks; the glittering but empty parade of masks. And my life becomes a front.

I idly chatter with you in the suave tones of surface talk.

I tell you everything that's really nothing; nothing of what's crying within me. So when I'm going through my routine, don't be fooled by what I'm not saying. Please listen carefully and try to hear what I'm not saying; what I'd like to be able to say; what for survival, I need to say but I can't. I dislike the hiding, honestly I do. I dislike the superficial, phony games I'm playing.

I'd really like to be genuine, spontaneous, and me. But you have to help me. You have to help me by holding out your hand, even when that's the last thing I seem to want or need. Each time you are kind, gentle and encouraging; each time you try to understand because you really care, my heart begins to grow wings; very small wings, very feeble wings, but wings. With your sensitivity, sympathy and power of understanding, I can make it. You can breathe life into me. I will not be easy for you. A long conviction of worthlessness builds strong walls. But love is stronger than strong walls and therein lies my hope. Please try to take down those walls with firm but gentle hands; for a child is very sensitive and I am a child. You may wonder: Who am I? I am every man, woman and child; every human you meet.

—Anonymous

Anxiety and difficulties can sometimes lead us to God or to our higher power. When we are in the throes of physical or emotional pain we frequently turn to God. In his book, *Finding Serenity in the Age of Anxiety*, Robert Gerzon, a psychotherapist, states "Anxiety is the back door to God's house. Love is the front door, but most of us feel too unworthy of love or too proud to admit we need it and we pass by that imposing and majestic entrance. But in his infinite compassion, God made a back door, so that if we missed the entrance we could always find our way in."

If our minds can create negative thoughts, they can also create positive thoughts. I love the poster of the "Little Engine That Could," with the saying, "If a stupid little train can do it, you can do it too!"

Your assignments for this chapter:

1. Gratitude:
    - Thanks, God, for helping me control my temper.
    - Thanks, God, for helping me forgive.
    - Thanks for helping me trust in thee.
    - I now release any anger or hatred I might carry.

2. Memorize the following affirmations:
    - I now forgive all people who need forgiving.
    - I am letting go of all the fears, stress, and anxiety I have been holding onto.

*People can alter their lives
by altering their attitudes.*

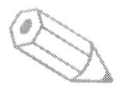

11
Managing Stress

*Things are neither good nor bad,
but thinking makes them so.*

—Shakespeare

The Physical Results of Stress

Stress is an everyday occurrence in life. You can't avoid it. A little stress can give you energy and invigorate your mind, but too much stress can quicken your breathing, make your heart beat faster, cause your blood pressure to rise, can change your brain chemistry, and can create excessive stress hormones.

Pessimistic and stressful thinking sets off a chain of disregulation in your neurotransmitters which can upset the neurochemicals released by your hypothalamus which can lead to an imbalance of your pituitary hormones and an excess of cortisol from your adrenal cortex. University studies have confirmed that depressed persons have more cortisol in their systems than others that are not depressed.

Stress can be caused by unhappy relationships, work, money problems, loud noises, too many major life changes, and other factors. Stress is the body's response to that which seems threatening or challenging. Too much stress for too long can lead to depression and mental and physical exhaustion. The most damaging emotional stress is when you feel you have no options, choices, or alternatives. We all differ in our response to stress; the right amount of stress for one person could be too much for another.

Take Positive Steps to Reduce Stress

The best stress remedies are those that help you to manage your stress levels yourself. When you can't change the situation, you can change your attitude and your internal self-talk. Learn to be an optimist rather than a pessimist. Take positive steps to reduce the stress in your life by avoiding too many major life changes all at once, using creative visualizations, deep breathing, exercise, mindfulness, getting the proper rest and nutrition, taking breaks, and doing things you enjoy.

Following are some activities you can choose to help you alleviate stress:

Visualization

It would be an understatement to say that there was considerable stress involved when we put two families (five teenagers) together. One day while meditating in a quiet chapel with my eyes closed, I suddenly visualized all of my difficulties being wrapped in a clean white parcel that resembled a rolled-up Sunday newspaper. The parcel fell off my lap, rolled out of the chapel, down the sidewalk, into the gutter and out onto the street, where a delivery truck ran over the parcel and smashed it into oblivion, and then my troubles were gone. It felt great. An elephant had been lifted off my back. This wasn't a visualization I created, it was like a daydream.

You can create your own visualizations.

Deep Breathing

Correct breathing is one of the best ways to "quiet the mind" and balance your equilibrium. When you breathe, you normally use chest or thoracic breathing, or you breathe from your diaphragm or abdomen. Chest or thoracic breathing is usually associated with anxiety or emotional stress. Abdominal breathing is the natural breathing of newborn babies and sleeping adults. Typically, most people breathe from 18,000 to 24,000 breaths a day, totally unaware of even one of those breathing cycles. Breathing exercises can be learned in a matter of minutes.

Thich Nhat Hanh said, "Our breath is the bridge from our body to our mind."

During my treatment for liver cancer, one of the first things my doctor assigned me to do was twenty minutes of deep breathing every day.

You may want to slowly record the following instructions and listen to them as you start your breathing exercises. You may also have someone read them to you.

Begin by lying flat or sitting comfortably, with one hand placed on your stomach just below your navel and the other hand on the center of your chest. Close your eyes. Notice how you are breathing. Which hand rises the most as you inhale? Are you breathing from your diaphragm or chest?

Now, lie on a rug or blanket, or on the floor, or on a firm mattress. Bend your knees and move your feet about eight inches apart.

Place one hand on the abdomen and one hand on your chest. Inhale slowly and deeply through your nose and feel the air flow into your abdomen to push your hand up as much as feels comfortable. Exhale. Smile slightly and inhale through your nose, exhale through your mouth as though you were letting out a deep sigh or whooshing sound. Your jaw and body should be relaxed.

Take a deep breath; inhale deeply until you feel your belly rising. Hold it for a few seconds and then exhale deeply. Repeat for five minutes (use your timer) and gradually work up to twenty minutes a day. To release tension, as you inhale, say to yourself, "Relaxation." As you exhale, breath out, and say "Tension."

To stimulate alertness, sit or stand straight, inhale a natural breath and hold it for a few seconds. Pretend that you are blowing through a straw and exhale a little air with substantial force through the small opening between your lips. Stop exhaling for a moment, then blow out more air in small, forceful puffs.

Repeat for several minutes. As you breath, imagine that energy is flowing out to all parts of your body with each exhalation.

Progressive Relaxation

Our body frequently responds to anxiety, stressful thoughts and challenging events with muscle tension. Muscle tension increases anxiety. Deep muscle relaxation reduces physiological tension and alleviates anxiety. You may want to record or have someone read the following muscle relaxation exercise to you.

Begin by lying on a bed or on a comfortable lounge chair. You may open or close your eyes. I prefer my eyes closed. Slowly open your mouth, and move your jaw gently from side to side, close your mouth, take a deep breath and slowly blow the air out. Tense every muscle in your body, eyes, arms, hands, back, stomach, legs and feet. Hold the tension for ten seconds and then let go. Feel the release and calmness come over you. Tighten your right fist and loosen all other muscles until they are limp; hold your fist for seven seconds, relax for twenty seconds. Each muscle or muscle grouping will be tensed for five to seven seconds and then relaxed for twenty to thirty seconds.

Keeping the rest of your body relaxed, tighten your forehead. The deeper you tighten your muscles, the more relaxed they will become. Now relax and let go. Feel the tension moving out.

Squint your eyes tightly and feel the tension around your eyes, then relax and let go.

Take a deep breath and hold it and then silently say, "Relax and let go" as you breathe out.

Tighten your jaw, then relax and let go.

Close your mouth and push your tongue against the roof or your mouth and feel the tension in your mouth. Relax and let go.

Do this with the top of your head, forehead, eyes, jaws, cheeks, and neck, and make sure these muscles are relaxed.

Give your entire body a chance to relax, then breathe in and fill your lungs to capacity. Hold your breath and notice the tension. Exhale, and relax.

Tighten your shoulder muscles, hold for seven seconds, relax and breathe out. Continue by tightening your arms. Then tighten your hands, elbows, stomach, thighs, buttocks, shins, knees, calves, ankles and feet.

Curl your toes downward, feel the tension in your calves, relax. Bend your toes toward your face, relax. Feel the relaxation in your toes, ankles, calves, shins, knees, and buttocks. Feel it spread to your abdomen, chest, shoulders, neck, arms, hands, head, jaw, and eyes.

With practice, you will be able to use progressive relaxation whenever you begin to feel stress. At the first sign of anxiety, scan your body for muscle tension, then do a quick progressive relaxation.

Exercise

Vigorous exercise is one of the most effective means of stress reduction. It returns your body to its normal equilibrium by releasing natural chemicals which help combat the stress. Aerobic exercises, such as jogging, swimming, walking, dancing, and biking, can generate a significant antidepressant effect.

Plan your own exercising program, but spend twenty minutes or more a day in continuous uninterrupted exercise. Brisk walking is as effective as any other exercise. If you're unmotivated, join a spa, an exercise group or aerobic class, or find a friend to walk with you. If it's too cold to walk outside, try walking at a mall. Most malls open at 5 or 6 a.m. to accommodate people.

Gaining Control of Your Time and Your Life

To manage your time and your life more effectively, arrange your activities so that most of your energy is spent on what is most important to you. Minimize time spent on activities you don't value highly. Set goals to accomplish the things you want to do in your life. Each evening, write down in a day planner or notebook ten things you would like to accomplish the following day. Scan the list and choose your number-one priority, then your number two, number three, and then number the entire list. As you accomplish your tasks each day, cross the item off your list. It doesn't matter if you accomplish all ten tasks; the important item is that you are working on your priority goals.

Remember that 20 percent of what you do will produce 80 percent of your rewards. Use that time wisely. You don't have to answer every phone call, read every piece of junk mail, or read the entire newspaper each day—you can scan the newspaper.

Simplify your life. Take time to smell the roses.

Set short-range goals that will frame your long-range priorities. Be flexible. Establish a reward for yourself when you accomplish a significant goal.

Use a day-timer or a week-at-a-glance calendar to help you take small steps towards accomplishing your goals.

Create a place of serenity in your home, a sanctuary of peace and healing. It's up to you to decide if you're going to be a stress seeker or a stress handler.

Secrets of a Good Night's Sleep

Insomnia is frequently a symptom of anxiety and stress. There are several different types of insomnia that people suffer. First, there is *sleep onset insomnia*, which is characterized by the inability to fall asleep. Second, *maintenance insomnia* is the inability to stay asleep, and third, early *morning insomnia*, which is waking up very early and not being able to return to sleep.

Normally, most people fall asleep within seven to fifteen minutes after their head hits the pillow. For those with difficulty falling asleep, try the deep breathing exercises that are mentioned above. Breathe in peaceful sleep, breathe out insomnia; repeat until you feel drowsy. Count backwards from one-hundred (or five-hundred)... 100, 99, 98, 97.... Buy a calm, serene, relaxing tape that will soothe you to sleep. I like the alpine stream, but you may prefer soft music or ocean sounds.

Don't drink caffeine, or if you do, don't drink it after 4 p.m. because all caffeine-containing products make sleeping difficult.

Some studies suggest that lack of major nutrients can cause sleep problems.

You may want to consider taking trace minerals—calcium is especially important because it has a calming effect on the central nervous system. The recommended dosage is anywhere from 800 to 1500 milligrams daily. Consult your health professional about what dosage is best for you. In addition, magnesium, Vitamin B-3 (niacin), Vitamin B-6, and Vitamin B-12 have been used to successfully treat depression.

Herbs that have been used to treat insomnia include hops, lady slipper, passion flower, skullcap, chamomile, and valerian root.

Foods such as bananas, figs, dates, yogurt, tuna, turkey, and whole-grain crackers are all high in tryptophan and will help promote sleep. Some studies have found that even small doses of melatonin (a sleep-inducing hormone) induces sleep for many people.

Again, consult your health care professional.

If you wake up in the middle of the night and have difficulty falling back to sleep, try the deep breathing exercises and counting backward. If that doesn't work, get up and quietly read, work on a craft such as needlepoint, write or watch television until you're tired. A lack of calcium and magnesium can cause you to wake up in the middle of the night. In addition, a deficiency of copper and iron can cause insomnia. A hair analysis can determine what your body is lacking.

Early morning insomnia may be due to depression or too much light in your room. Adjust the curtains or lighting in your room so that it is darker.

Each evening I place a tape in my cassette player and fall asleep to the cerebral sounds of an alpine stream.

Mindfulness

Mindfulness is the art of getting the most out of the present moment. Live in the present. Most of our anxiety comes from thinking about the past or worrying about the future. If you are focused on what you are doing right now, there is no room for fear, worry, anxiety, anger, or any other stressful emotions. Remember that constant anxiety or stress can cause depression, so the less stress, the less depression.

David Cooper wrote, "In the Western traditions, mindfulness is associated with devotional practices in which the Divine is a constant companion within us. In Christianity, the practice is having Jesus by your side at all times. In Judaism, the cabalistic idea that creation is taking place in each and every moment brings an acute sensitivity to everything. All of these ideas can be practiced to raise our level of awareness and induce an entirely new perspective, seeing things "as they really are."

Don't hang on to experiences, events or people from the past. "Hanging on to resentment is allowing someone you despise to live rent free in your head."

Because I am a Type "A" personality, I am frequently thinking about all of the things I need and want to do next instead of living in the present moment and finding pleasure in that moment. Stress is often the result of trying to do too much at once, and always being in a hurry.

Begin mindfulness with deep breathing and become very aware of each breath you take. Notice your breath as you inhale, then as you exhale. Count each breath.

Practice mindfulness while you eat. Observe the color, texture, and shape of your food. Does it have an aroma? Does it perk your taste buds? What smells do you recognize? When you take your first bite, feel your teeth piercing the food. Chew slowly. What are you tasting? When thoughts arise, notice them, then return your attention to eating the food.

Too often in our daily activities we are on automatic pilot and are only going through the motions of living. Practice living for one hour in the present moment. When other thoughts come rushing into your mind, notice them, and then come back to the present moment and everything you are experiencing in the here-and-now. Each day increase the time spent in mindfulness until you are living in the precious moment that is now.

Jerry Braza, in his book, *Mindfulness* wrote, "Mindfulness is experiencing the body, mind, and spirit in the same place at the same time."

Yoga

Yoga means to be united with your soul and the "One who gave you the soul." My preference is Kundalini Yoga, which is referred to as the creative potential of man or woman. It is a powerful tool for expanding awareness. I will discuss only a few highlights of Kundalini. If you can, it would be helpful to take a class in Kundalini yoga, or buy a book or video tape. I like the book, *Kundalini Yoga, the Flow of Eternal Power*, by Shakti Parwha Kaur Khaslsa, Ph.D.

As you may recall, in an earlier chapter I discussed music and healing and mentioned Don Campbell being healed by "balancing the tones" in his body. We all have energy—we live in a sea of energy. In the book *Kundalini Yoga*, Shakti Khalsa writes, "There is a particular vibratory frequency corresponding to every sound in the universe." When you watch your favorite television show, you have to select the right channel. Tuning into your correct channel is simply changing channels on the television of your mind and in yoga, this is done with a mantra. Each day you choose, either consciously or unconsciously, programs that play on the screen of your mind by the thoughts you think and words you speak. Both thoughts and words have energy and vibrations. To create the vibration for this exercise you will begin with the mantra,"Ong Namo Guru Dev Namo," meaning "I bow to the Creator, to the Divine teacher within."

Begin by sitting cross-legged on the floor with your spine straight. You can sit on a chair, but make sure both feet are on the floor. Place the palms of your hands together at the center of your chest and place your thumbs firmly but lightly at the center of your sternum, fingers pointing upward.

Take several deep breaths, inhaling through the nose, then exhale entirely through the nose. Repeat this several times. Inhale deeply through the nose and vibrate the syllable "Ong" at the back of your throat, and sense the sound going out through the nose. Continue chanting the rest of the mantra, Ong Namo Guru Dev Namo. Dev rhymes with save. Chant from your navel point and repeat the mantra until you feel "connected." The melody is not as important as the rhythm and the breath. Chanting stimulates the 84 pressure points in the roof of the mouth and this creates positive changes in brain chemistry. Breathe in energy and feel yourself being filled with life, light and joy. Feel your breath carry away tension, fatigue, worry and disease.

Most people breathe fifteen times per minute, but when breathing becomes more rapid and irregular, the mind also becomes more erratic and disturbed. It is the intricate essence of the breath that contains our life energy, which is called prana. If you can change the rate of your breathing, you can calm your mind, and you can do that by increasing your lung capacity. This can be done by "Breath of Fire," which is done by rapid and powerful breathing through your nose. Breathe rapidly through your nose with your mouth closed. Start out slowly and pick up speed until you're breathing 120 to 180 times per minute. Imagine you are making the sounds of a steam engine going uphill. Don't pause or hold your breath, but do one long continuous breath. This will take practice. Long deep breathing will harmonize the body, mind and spirit.

When you breathe less than eight times per minute, you stimulate the secretion of your pituitary gland, which is the control panel for your intuition and will increase your inner guidance. It will take daily practice to help strengthen your lungs and slow your breathing.

Your right nostril controls your energy level and the left controls your emotions. If you're agitated, depressed, angry, emotionally disturbed, or stressed, you can calm your nervous system by placing the thumb of the right hand on the right nostril and closing the nostril. Do long and deep breathing through the left nostril for about five minutes.

One day after I had been hurrying around, I went to the pharmacy to pick up a prescription for my husband. While waiting, I took my blood pressure. My resting pulse was 107. I closed my right nostril and took deep breaths through my left nostril. Within two minutes my pulse was down to 93.

You can energize and calm the nervous system by breathing through the right nostril and closing off the left nostril. Do this for about five minutes.

Yoga is a very powerful and ancient system of stress management. Patanjali compiled the first system of yoga between 5,000 B.C. and 300 A.D. Yoga is not a religion, but a method to enhance, heal, clear the mind, energize, open the chakras, increase consciousness and broaden your present experience. Most of the visualization, relaxation, and meditation techniques we use today are derived from yoga.

Keep a Gratitude Journal

Even in ancient times, people were admonished to express gratitude. In Psalms 106:1, David wrote, "Praise ye the Lord. O give thanks unto the Lord; for he is good: for his mercy endureth forever." And again, in Ephesians 5:20, "Give thanks always for all things unto God . . ."

Almost nothing brings me closer to God than expressing my gratitude to Him for the blessings that he has given me. Have you ever given a special gift to someone—a gift that you thought was a wonderful present, but the recipient didn't even thank you? Were you a little offended that you had spent so much time and effort, yet received no thanks? I think God or our Higher Power may be offended when we fail to thank Him for the bounteous blessings in our lives—sunrise, sunsets, trees, rivers, forests, mountains, blue sky, rain, flowers, fruits, the song of a bird, hearing, sight, legs, hands, the giggle of a baby, the playfulness of a puppy, a healthy heart—the list could go on forever. When I see what my husband endures with dialysis, I am so grateful for my kidneys.

Learned Optimism

You can learn to be an optimist. Long ago Epictetus wrote, "Man is not disturbed by events, but by the view he takes of them."

While teaching a group of high school students about stress management and positive thinking, I asked how many were optimists. Less than a third of the students raised their hands. Two-thirds of the students claimed to be pessimists. Obviously, there was a lot of "stinking-thinking" or cognitive distortion among them.

First, I worked with their irrational assumptions that things were "being done to them" and that they had no control over their lives, or that the external world controlled their life. I taught them that someone else doesn't make you angry, you choose to be angry or offended. You have control over what you feel or experience. If you are angry or resentful at someone, you are letting that person live rent free in your head.

Next time you think negative, place an elastic around your wrist, and when unwanted thoughts come up, snap the elastic and say out loud or to yourself, "Stop. When I talk negative to myself, I feel terrible, and that is not the way I want to feel." You can also gently pinch yourself when you think negative. Change every negative thought into a positive thought. Try to see the positive side of everything.

When you have bad things happen, ask yourself what you have learned from the experience that will help you or others in the future. Realize that without difficulties, we do not grow. Everything you are experiencing is for your growth.

Use a piece of graph paper and chart it for one month. On the left-hand side of the paper, write numbers from one to ten, with the number ten at the top of the paper and number one on the bottom. By the number ten, write optimism. By number one, write pessimism. Each day put a mark on the graph or draw a smiley face on your level of optimism. Try to find ways each day to improve your optimism.

Remember, when you realize that what you think about becomes your reality, you become very careful about what you think about.

At the end of each chapter I have assigned you to write down something you were thankful for each day. Make this a daily habit for the rest of your life; write down five things that you are grateful for each morning or evening.

Your assignments for this chapter:

1. Exercise five times a week for twenty minutes.

2. Practice mindfulness each day.

3. Spend five to twenty minutes a day doing deep breathing exercises.

4. Keep a daily gratitude journal.

5. Memorize and repeat these affirmations daily:
   - Everyday in every way, I am an optimist.
   - In every situation I choose my reaction.
   - Happiness is a process I create, not a product of fate.

*Being at peace with yourself
is a direct result of
finding peace with God.*

12
Connecting With Your Higher Power

*Peace I leave with you, my peace I give unto you:
not as the world giveth, give I unto you.
Let not your heart be troubled,
neither let it be afraid.*

—John 14:27

Help Is Available from On High

A power higher than ourselves can sustain and lift us. Help is available, if we are willing to risk believing in that power and solicit spiritual succorance.

When I first found out I had liver cancer, I was determined to take Bernie Seagul's advice and spend the rest of my life "living," not dying. My mind pondered the things I wanted to do: Leave a legacy of letters for my children and grandchildren. Write my obituary. Do some genealogy. Once, during my contemplations, I entered a church and came face-to-face with an impressive portrait of the Savior. Since I was all alone, I took time to pause and look into the eyes of the portrait. I stood there for some time, caught up in the serenity and the majesty I felt. Then I heard Him say to me, in that still small voice within, "You're going to be okay, Pat." An over-powering peace cascaded through my body like a warm shower. I knew I was going to be okay. That was the beginning of my healing. I no longer thought about writing an obituary or dying. Three months later my cancer was in remission. I didn't do chemotherapy—my immune system was already in jeopardy because of the chronic fatigue syndrome. I chose instead, alternative medicine and became a vegetarian—almost vegan.

Wayne Dyer says that if we knew who walks beside us, we would not be afraid.

An Old Testament story tells of an incredible chase scene: the prophet Elisha and his servant were pursued by a huge Syrian army that had surrounded the entire city. Trembling with fright, the young servant lad asked Elisha, "What shall we do?" and Elisha answered, "Fear not: for those that be with us are greater than those that be with them."

Now, you can imagine the thoughts of the servant, "Here we are all alone on this mountain, surrounded by the biggest army I've ever seen, and this old man thinks there are people here to help us. Man, we're in big trouble."

Elisha, perhaps perceiving the lad's thoughts, prays, "Lord, open his eyes that he might see." And the Lord opened the eyes of the young man; and he saw: and behold the mountain was full of horses and chariots of fire around Elisha. (2 Kings 6:15-18) The Lord fought the battle for them.

Even in our day, for the righteous, those that be with us are greater than those that be with them. "Fear not, I am with thee."

Reach for the Light!

Upon a cabinet inside my home rests a splendid green fern, with one side facing a distant window. The portion of the fern nearest the window is more lush, and sixteen inches taller than the side not reaching for the light. When you reach for the light—your higher power, your soul becomes more luminous, more radiant, and expands accordingly. There is a divine energy within every living soul, and this energy permeates all that is in the universe.

In the book of Genesis, chapter 1, verse 26, we are told that we are created in God's image. "And God said, Let us make man in our image, after our likeness." Many religions echo this belief. Hinduism espouses the belief that God lives within you as you. Buddhism declares, "Look within you, you are the Buddha." Christianity teaches ". . . the kingdom of God is within you." (Luke 17:21.) In other words you are a God in embryo, you are in the process of becoming like God, depending on how you live your life.

In his book, *Manifest Your Destiny*, and while discussing divine energy, Wayne Dyer quotes Bhagavad Gita:

> He who sees that the Lord of all is ever the same in all that is—immortal in the field of mortality—he sees the truth. And when a man sees that the God in himself is the same God that is in all that is, he hurts not himself by hurting others. Then he goes indeed, to the highest path.

Aid in Being Restored to Wholeness

A power greater than ourselves can restore us to wholeness. Take a moment now to go to the place that is peaceful within you. Shut your eyes and visualize yourself going to the place where your Higher Power dwells. Your Higher Power might be God, Jesus, Buddha, or whoever you worship. Give your problem or depression to your Higher Power. Thank this power for taking your problem and healing your depression.

If you are unable to go to the place where this power dwells, imagine a large container and begin filling it with all of the reasons you are unable to go. As soon as it is full, empty the container of all the contents and return to the place where your Higher Power dwells. Give your problems and depression to this power and offer thanks. As you do this, you will be free to use your energy to help others and contribute to the universe.

Swami Vivekananda, a spiritual teacher in the 1890's, spoke of the divinity within each of us. He said, "In one word, this ideal is that you are divine . . . To many this is . . . a terrible ideal, and most think it can never be reached; but it can be realized by everyone. . . . nothing will stand as a bar to the realization of this ideal, because it is realized already. All the powers in the universe are already ours. It is we who have put our hands before our eyes and cry that it is dark. Know that there is no darkness around you. Take your hands away and there is the light which was from the beginning."

Prayers Are Often Answered through Others

It has been said that God answers our prayers, but it is usually through another that he meets our needs.

Leigh Lunt, in her beautiful poem, *Abou Ben Adhem*, sums up the process of losing ourselves:

Abou Ben Adhem

Abou Ben Adhem (may his tribe increase)
Awoke one night from a deep dream of peace,
And saw, within the moonlight in his room,
Making it rich, and like a lily in bloom,
An angel writing in a book of gold:—
Exceeding peace had made Ben Adhem bold,
And to the presence in the room he said,
"What writest thou?" —The vision raised its head,
And with a look made of all sweet accord,
Answered, "The names of those who love the Lord."
"And is mine one?" said Abou. "Nay, not so,"
Replied the angel. Abou spoke more low,
But cheerily still; and said, " I pray thee then,
Write me as one who loves his fellow-men."
The angel wrote and vanished. The next night
It came again, with a great wakening light,
And showed the names whom love of God had blessed,
And lo! Ben Adhem's name led all the rest.

Blessings Come From Service to Others

If we expect blessings from God, we must serve our fellow men. You can't pray cream and live skim milk. Mother Teresa was a wonderful example of losing her life by serving others.

As Jesus was about to depart his mortal ministry, he assured his disciples, "I will not leave you comfortless . . . I will pray the Father, and he shall give you another Comforter, that he may abide with you for ever, even the Spirit of truth; . . . He shall teach you all things and bring all things to your remembrance . . ." (John 14:16)

Many people do not hear the voice, others do not want to hear the voice. If we are preoccupied we may not hear it at all.

So often we plead to the Lord or to a higher power to answer some prayer "Please let this happen . . ." instead of having the faith to thank Him ahead of time for blessings we want to come into our life. So often we're afraid to "Let go and let God help us."

The following poem was given to me by a woman in one of my support groups.

> THE NEED TO TRUST
> As children bring their broken toys
>   With tears for us to mend,
> I brought my broken dreams to God
>   Because he was my friend.
> But then instead of leaving Him
>   In peace to work alone,
> I hung around and tried to help in ways
>   That were my own.
> At last I snatched them back and cried,
>   "How could you be so slow?"
> "My child," he said, "What could I do?"
>   "You never would let go."

Hopelessness can dissipate as we learn to trust God. In his book, *The Golden Present*, Swami Satchidananda discusses the mechanism of devotion, prayer, and selfless service.

> Don't think that you can do everything by your own capacity alone. Know that there is a higher power, a grace, to help you; but you have to sincerely ask for it. Unless you ask, you won't receive it. Just by asking you are opening yourself to that power. It's not that God is

waiting for you to ask; God is not miserly. He is already giving, but we do not always receive.

The process of asking is itself opening; you cannot even ask without opening. So open your heart. Even if you can't open your heart to people, open your heart to God; then you will know how to open your heart to people also. Pray sincerely and trust in a higher power, trust in God. Many, many more things are wrought by prayer than the world dreams of.

You might have the entire world at your feet . . . ; but unless you have peace you don't have a worriless life. . . . If you have peace, even without having anything else you will be happy. Accept God's will: "Whatever has to come will come. What will not come, will not come. Why should I worry about it?"

. . . All you have to accomplish is to see that all selfishness goes away.

Turning Your Problems Over to God

Pray to God, but row toward shore. When I was a coordinator of a women's center we scheduled a dinner at the home of one of the women in our group. When I arrived a few minutes early she showed me a small box. "See this box?" she said. "Everything—any problem I can do something about, I do. But when I can't do something about it, I turn it over to God. He's going to be up all night anyway." She then started pulling out tiny slips of paper with writing on them. "In the last year he has taken care of almost every problem in my box."

Socrates, while commenting on the medical history of his day, said, "While it is not proper to cure the eyes without the head, nor the head without the body; so neither is it proper to cure the body without the soul."

Your assignments for this chapter:

1. Get a small box or envelope and turn the problems that you can't do anything about over to God, or to your Higher Power.

2. Visit or attend a church, temple or synagogue.

3. Listen to uplifting music and read good poetry.

4. Pray and meditate several times a day.

5. Listen to the inner or still small voice within you.

6. Pray every day that you might touch the lives of others so that they might live closer to their higher power.

7. Gratitude:
- I am grateful for guidance from a higher power.
- I am grateful for the healing that comes from connecting with my higher power.
- I am grateful for scriptures and other spiritual writings that uplift and guide me in my life.
- I am grateful for guardian angels.

8. Memorize and repeat these affirmations daily:
- I trust God to help and guide me each day.
- I am a child of God on a divinely appointed earthly mission.
- I delight in divine love from my higher power.

*The secret of happiness
is not in doing what one likes to do,
but in liking what one has to do.*

—Sir James M. Barrie

13
Enduring and Persevering

*Hope is the thing with feathers—
That perches in the soul—
And sings the tune without the words—
And never stops—at all—*

—Emily Dickinson

Life's Journey: "Hang Ups and Bang Ups"

Some of the great men and women in history have persevered even when they wanted to give up. Sometimes the only way through a problem is to "work through" it. Robert Lewis Stevensen wrote, "I have willed that my battlefield shall be the dingy, inglorious, one of the bed and medicine bottle. For fourteen years I have not had a day of real health. I have wakened sick and gone to bed weary, yet I have done my work unflinchingly. I have written in bed and out of bed, written in hemorrhages, written in sickness, written torn by coughing, written when my head swam for weakness—and I have done it all for so long that it seems to me that I have won my wager and recovered my glove. Yet, the battle still goes on: ill or well is a trifle so long as it goes. I was made for contest, and the Powers-That-Be sustained me."

Life is full of mountains and valleys. Most crises do pass, but until they do, what is your plan to stay centered? Dr. Suess has a wonderful book, *Oh The Places You'll Go* . . . , that I like to read to my grandchildren and even to groups of high school students. I like to think of the book as a resilient flexibility journey through life. It describes the journey of "hang ups and bang ups" that will happen to you, but in the end you can move mountains.

I recall a high-stress day when my seven children were young, restless, quarreling, and fogged in by drenching rain. In desperation I asked if they wanted to go for ice cream, hoping this would calm things down a little. They were elated, but then started arguing about whom got to sit by the window. "Just get in the car," I said. "If there's one more argument, we won't go." Then the telephone rang for me.

Anticipating the horrendous commotion I might find in the car after a fifteen-minute telephone conversation, I considered staying home. Much to my surprise, as I hopped in the car all was quiet. Then it happened. One of the most tender scenes a mother could encounter. Shari had smuggled her guitar into the car and as I looked into the rear view mirror my gang of kids began singing. I pinched myself to see if it was a dream. No, it was really my crew in collaborative concert. I hadn't heard so much harmony since the last Barbershop Quartet Contest. I'd heard the song before, but never really listened to the words.

". . . Everyone knows that ants can't move a rubber tree plant," and then . . . "Ooops there goes another rubber tree plant. High hopes, I've got high in the sky, apple pie hopes . . ."

It really had a message. One ant can't move a rubber tree plant, but a bunch of ants could. One family member couldn't create harmony, but a family working . . . singing . . . together could.

The Joy of Life Is the Trip

Strive to live in the present moment and realize that each minute is a miraculous gift from God. "Yesterday is gone, tomorrow is not here, today is the journey." The following story illustrates this point:

The Station

Tucked away in our subconscious mind is an idyllic vision. We see our selves on a long trip that spans the continent. We are traveling by train. Out of the windows we drink in the passing scene of children waving at a crossing, of cattle grazing on a distant hillside, and of mountains and rolling hills.

But uppermost in our minds is the final destination. On a certain day at a certain hour we will pull into the station. Bands will be playing and flags waving. Once we get there so many wonderful dreams will come true and the pieces of our lives will fit together like a completed jigsaw puzzle. How restlessly we pace the aisles—waiting, waiting for the station.

When we reach the station, that will be it! We cry, "When I put the last kid through college. When I have paid off the mortgage! When I get a promotion! When I finish school! When I reach the age of retirement, I shall live happily ever after!"

Sooner or later we must realize there is no station, no place to arrive at once and for all. The true joy of life is the trip. The station is only a dream. It constantly outdistances us.

Relish the moment. It isn't the burdens of today that drive men mad. It is the regrets over yesterday and the fear of tomorrow. Regret and fear are the twin thieves who rob us of today.

So stop pacing the aisles and counting the miles. Instead, climb more mountains, go barefoot more often, swim more rivers, watch more sunsets, laugh more, cry less. Life will be lived as we go along. The station will come soon enough.

—Robert J. Hastings

Advice from Psalm 118:24 is still applicable today: "This is the day the Lord hath made; we will rejoice and be glad in it."

We're Here to See One Another Through

Renoir, one of the great artists in history, suffered from an advanced rheumatism during his later life, particularly in his hands. When a friend stopped by to see the aging painter, he noticed that every brush stroke was causing the artist great pain. The friend asked Renoir, "Why is it that you still have to work? Why do you continue to torture yourself?" Renoir slowly answered, "The pain passes, but the pleasure, the beauty of creation, remains."

In enduring and helping others endure, I like the advice, "We are not here to see through one another, but to see one another through."

When we busy ourselves in good works, we don't have time to be depressed. "He who rows the boat doesn't have time to rock it."

Avoid Self-Pity and Self-Contempt

Often I have counseled young people or adults that they are where they are in life because that's where they want to be. There is an emotional pay-off for being negative or depressed. Sometimes they get more attention from their parents or friends. Oscar Wilde said, "There is luxury in self-contempt. When we demean ourselves we feel others have no right to criticize us." Sometimes there is luxury in self-pity. We don't have to move on or take responsibility to improve our life or help others because we have too many problems of our own. "If we lock ourselves in a jail of self-pity, we are the jailer who holds the keys."

>   THE OLD FROG
> Once on the edge of a quiet pool,
> Under the bank where 'twas nice and cool,
> Just where the stream flowed out of the bay,
> There sat a grumpy and mean old frog,
> Who sat all day in the sand to soak,
> And just did nothing but croak and croak,
> A blackbird hollered, "I say you know,
> Are you in trouble or pain or what?"
> The old frog growled, "Mine is an awful lot,
> Tis a dirty world," thus the old frog spoke.
> "Croakety, croakety, croakety, croak."
> Then the blackbird said, "I see what's wrong.
> Why don't you smile or sing a song"
> Look up, young feller, well bless my soul,
> You're looking down a muskrat hole!"
> A wise old turtle, who boarded near,
> Said to the blackbird, "Now friend see here,
> Don't waste no tears on him," says he.
> That fool's down there, cause he wants to be."

There is wise advice in the alcoholics' serenity prayer. "God grant me the serenity to accept the things I cannot change, the courage to change the things I can, and the wisdom to know the difference."

"If you expect to leave footprints in the sands of time, you had better wear work shoes."

Press On

A gifted spiritual leader gave this advice about depression: "Pressing on even though surrounded by a cloud of depression, will eventually bring you out into the sunshine."

One of my favorite quotes, a statement by Calvin Coolidge, is: "Press on: Nothing in the world can take the place of persistence. Talent will not; nothing is more common than unsuccessful individuals with talent. Genius will not; unrewarded genius is almost a proverb. Education will not; the world is full of educated derelicts. Persistence and determination alone are omnipotent."

Your assignments for this chapter:

1. Select and read or skim through a biography of someone who has overcome adversity or depression. The list could include Abraham Lincoln, Golda Meir, Margret Thatcher, Joan Of Arc, Benjamin Franklin, Walt Disney, and on-and-on.

2. Write down several significant things about yourself you would like said in your obituary.

3. Pick a bouquet of dandelions or sunflowers. If it's winter, gather up some pine boughs or pine cones and place them in a basket in your home.

4. Read to a child.

5. Sing and rock a baby to sleep.

6. Play with a puppy.

7. Gratitude:
   - I am grateful for today, and for what yesterday has taught me.
   - I am grateful for forests, lakes, and a wondrous world.
   - I give thanks for all the good things I have, and for all of the good things that will come into my life.

8. Memorize and repeat these affirmations daily:
   - I love the world, and this love returns to me.
   - Life is fun, and I am willing to enjoy it.
   - Just for today, I will live five minutes at a time.
   - I will see beauty and goodness in each precious moment.
   - The world is a beautiful place to be.

14
Developing Personal Power

*No man can be at peace with his neighbor
who is not at peace with himself.*

—Edna St. Vincent Millay

Are you a doormat or a victim? Do you feel like a puppet on someone else's string? Are you a bully? Do you have little respect for the wants and needs of other people? Are you wishy-washy? If you answered "yes" to any of these questions, you may need assertiveness training.

Defining Assertive Behavior

Assertive behavior means standing up for your rights and expressing your feelings, thoughts, and beliefs in direct and honest ways without trampling on the rights of others.

An assertive person is able to express thoughts and feelings in a direct, honest and appropriate way in order to communicate expectations. He is able to deal effectively with others without dominating, humiliating or degrading the other person. He also is able to make or deny requests such as saying "No."

The Need for Personal Balance

While I think it's crucial that we serve others, it's essential that we maintain a balance in our own lives so we don't burn out. It's okay to say, "No," when we're exhausted, or when we just don't have the time to complete a task for someone else.

Imagine yourself lying on your back with 16 umbilical cords attached to your navel. All of the cords are stretching out to reach and connect to some needy person. Suddenly, someone wants to attach another cord. Do you say, "Go ahead and suck, I'm down to beetle juice anyway?" Or can you see yourself jumping up and down doing Indian war whoops, preparing to go to battle over your own navel?

Or, can you see yourself saying the line from the 23rd Psalm over and over again, "Yea, though I walk thru the valley of the shadow of death, I will fear no evil . . ."

A Self-Test

Circle the words that best describe you.

Passive	*Aggressive*	*Passive/Aggressive*	*Assertive*
self-pitying	rude	resentful	real
apologetic	insisting	spiteful	direct
victim	dominating	grudgeful	competent
doormat	pushy	bitter	energized
martyr	harsh	late	relaxed
timid	interrupting	sulky	powerful
injured	bossy	fearful	honest
helpless	preachy	anxious	centered
retreating	explosive	gossip	coping
withdrawn	domineering	phony	open
crying	thoughtless	sarcastic	flexible
sweet	mean	manipulative	confident
Stuck	Stuck	Stuck	Moving

Count the number of words you circled in each column. Are you passive, aggressive, passive/aggressive, or assertive? Because we do not always see ourselves objectively, have a friend or close relative circle the words they think best describe you and compare notes.

Notice at the bottom of each column, with the exception of the assertive list, the word "stuck." When you try to have a win-win relationship with a passive, aggressive, or passive/aggressive individual you are stuck.

Notice the word "moving" under the assertive column. A relationship can grow when two people are assertive. Where would you like to be?

On occasion I have counseled depressed women—people who were very "sweet," but inside they were seething because people took advantage of them all the time. When I suggested assertive training or saying "No" to unreasonable requests made by others, they were mortified and responded, "I can't say No, people will think I'm not a nice person." Somehow it seemed unchristian for them to take care of themselves. But Jesus was never a puppet on someone else's string. He was always in control of his own life. True, he was always ready and willing to do His Father's will and serve his fellowmen, but he didn't perform miracles to please the Sadducees or Pharisees. He did not always honor every request.

Don't misunderstand what I'm saying, because I believe as the Savior said, "... He that loseth his life for my sake, ... shall save it." (Luke 9:24). I think we should lose our life in service, but not at the expense of our health or well being.

Using "I" Messages

To become more assertive, it's important to understand the language you use when communicating. "I" messages usually indicate an assertive focus and communicate that you take responsibility for what you think and feel.

Using an "I" messages is learning to focus your communication onto what you know about, rather than on what you assume others know about you. For example, "I really enjoyed attending the basketball game with you."

When you are assertive, the message is that although you and I may have our differences, we are equally entitled to express our opinions to one another without violating each other's rights. For example:

Sheila: "I'm not comfortable attending another basketball game tonight."

Dan: "This is the biggest game of the year, and I really want to go."

Sheila: "Have you considered the option of asking your brother to go with you?"

Dan: "Great idea, I'll call him."

This is a win-win, flexible communication where both parties are open and honest and able to compromise.

Using the One-to-ten Scale

Another way to assess the wants and needs of another is to measure them on a scale of one-to-ten. Ten is good, one is undesirable.

Dan: "On a scale of one-to-ten, where are you on going to an adventure movie tonight?"

Sheila: "I'm at a two, but I'm at a ten for dancing."

Dan: "I'm at a one for dancing. How about bowling?"

Sheila: "Bowling sounds great."

Assertiveness does not guarantee winning, but it usually results in a compromise without making others angry. When we are assertive, we feel more self-confident and able to help others.

Passive Individuals

In contrast, passive individuals will usually withhold their wants, opinions and feelings. When you ask them what they want to do tonight they usually say, "I don't know." Passive individuals give up their rights and permit other people to "walk all over" them. They are constantly apologizing and doing what they are told, even when they don't want to. Often, they feel helpless, resentful, and anxious. Passive people usually try to please others and avoid conflict or rejection.

"You" messages are normally communication directed away from the speaker to the other person and indicate an aggressive focus. "You" messages accuse, blame, judge, or provoke another person. Frequently messages such as "You should," . . . "You will," . . . "You must," and "You ought," are attempts to control the other person or the situation by shifting responsibility away from the speaker onto the person being spoken to. For example, "You never help me," or "You are always late."

Aggressive Individuals

When we are aggressive the underlying message is, "I'm superior and always right and you're inferior." Aggressive individuals make enemies. The goals of an aggressive individual is to get some anger out of his system and dominate or humiliate others.

"We" messages often have a passive/aggressive or manipulative focus. The speaker doesn't want to take responsibility and projects it onto others. For example, "We need to have a party for our friends," or "We really made a big mistake." "We should never do that." A passive/aggressive individual may be sugary sweet to your face, yet be vicious when you're not around. They are usually phony, two-faced, cynical, sarcastic, and vengeful. Their goal is to manipulate or use others to their advantage. For example, "I don't think they will mind if we borrow their car."

Practice Role Playing

Learning to be assertive will take practice. Begin by practicing a conversation with yourself in the mirror. Remember that 75 to 80 percent of all communication is nonverbal. Your tone of voice, body language, eye contact, facial expressions, posture and gestures are all part of communication. Your tone of voice will either invite people into your space or stop them from invading it. If you are angry, defensive, hostile, or whiny, your message may not be heard. Even though your words may be assertive, if you're scowling, frowning or glaring, you're going to communicate anger. Look directly at yourself (or another person) without staring. Speak directly and distinctly so you can be easily heard. Watch your body language. Here is an is an example of a response to a friend who asks to borrow your car.

Madge: "Can I borrow your car over the weekend?"

You: "I don't feel comfortable lending my car."

Madge: "But I really need a car this weekend. It's an emergency. I have to take my friend skiing."

You: "I never lend my car."

Madge: "Please."

You: (smile and place your hand gently on her shoulder) "I don't lend my car."

Practice role playing the above scenario. Role-play some situations that you wished you had handled better. What would you say to a salesperson who is pressuring you to buy a car you can't afford? A simple statement like "No, I'm going to find a car that is within my budget," is adequate and should get the message across. Don't apologize when you say no. That opens the door for more arguments.

Sometimes you will find it necessary to refuse the request several times. "No." "No." This is frequently true with children or teenagers. A simple "No" is usually sufficient, but if it's an important relationship you may want to acknowledge what the other person is feeling such as, "I know you were hoping I could go with you and you may be disappointed, but I won't be able to go."

Three Parts of a Good Assertive Message

A good assertive message communicates (1) what you are feeling, and (2) why, and (3) what you would like. "I feel hurt when you are late because I worry that something might have happened to you. From now on, I would like you to call me when you are going to be late."

Avoid Victim Language

Do you use power or victim language? Following are some examples of victim language: My mother makes me angry. If it weren't for my husband I'd feel powerful. I could be more independent and do what I choose if it weren't for my roommate. I'd be a lot more successful if it weren't for my childhood. My neighbor makes me suspicious. My children make me lose my temper. I'd be more loving if my parents had given me more love. I'd make more money if I had a better boss. I'd be happier if it weren't for my surroundings.

Moving from Pessimism to Optimism

We are not born winners or losers, we are born choosers. No one else is responsible for our happiness, no one else can make us happy. Our husband or wife can't make us happy, our parents can't make us happy. We create our own happiness and sometimes, "thinking makes it so."

When I was teaching coping skills to about 500 high school students, I found that 75 percent of them were pessimists. I taught them about restructuring their negative thoughts into positive thoughts and gave them an optimist chart. At the top, I listed the dates for the days of the month. One the left hand side, I wrote the numbers from one to ten, beginning with one at the bottom at the page where I wrote the word "pessimist." At the top of the page I wrote the number ten and wrote "optimist" just above the number. I asked the students to put a dot on their level of optimism that day and asked them to work on becoming an optimist by changing every negative thought into a positive thought. When they had difficult times, I asked them to write down the good things they learned from challenge. I asked them to write down as many things as they could think of each day that they were grateful for and to focus on positive events in their life or things they normally took for granted like telephones, pencils, books and paper.

By the end of a month the students each had a graph about his or her level of optimism. Not only that, they took responsibility for becoming more positive and for their own behavior. They realized that they had power and control of their own life. The results were amazing. Grades improved, students were kinder to each other, there was a more positive attitude in the class room, and students gained a skill that could have a lasting impact. They felt centered and in control of their lives.

Being Centered and Maintaining Balance

When you are centered you are in control of your thoughts and feelings. Imagine yourself walking a tightrope and being perfectly balanced, then someone comes by and makes a comment that upsets you. You juggle to maintain your balance so you will not fall off the rope. It takes all of your energy and skill to stay on the rope.

What is it in your life that helps you maintain balance? What pulls you off balance? If you respond to the other person by getting angry, vengeful, or physical, and continue to dwell on the negative, you will fall. However, if you stay in the present moment with your thoughts focused on maintaining balance, you can make it to the end of the rope and safety. When you are centered you are in touch with your feelings and know what you want. You feel balanced, complete and whole.

Feelings such as fear, anger, and loneliness indicate what you like and don't like. Your thoughts include plans, ideas, and opinions and tell you what you want or don't want in your personal space. You are in control of your personal power when your feelings and thoughts are balanced and in harmony. For example, the other day I started to feel a tinge of jealousy and could feel my face becoming flushed and my heart beating faster. "What's going on here?" I asked myself. "This is not how I want to feel. It's stinking-thinking." I examined what I was telling myself, stopped the self-pity and then looked at the positive side of the situation. Within a few minutes I was okay.

Sometimes we let others pull us off balance when they use put-downs, borrow and not return, require us to meet their expectations, or they talk behind our back. Other times we pull ourselves off balance by putting things off, getting too tired or not eating properly, over-committing our time, or storing up negative feelings.

When you are not centered, take a deep breath (maybe block the right nostril and breathe deeply through the left nostril), and listen to what your body is saying. What are you feeling? What are you thinking or telling yourself? Is it rational? What do you want? Talk to yourself and take responsibility for what you want, who you are, what you can do, and what you will do to help the situation. For example, use statements like "I want to be centered. I enjoy being centered."

It's easy to be centered when life is calm and peaceful. When the battles of life confront you and runaway emotions and negative self-defeating thoughts erupt, let your inner wisdom bring you back to balance and harmony in your life.

Don't use words like, "I should... I ought to... I'll try... I wish... maybe... Don't project your power outside of yourself.

Responding to Criticism

Dealing with criticism can leave you defensive, angry, hostile, or in some cases grateful. If someone is criticizing you, relax and take a deep breath. Listen to what the other person is saying and try to repeat back what he has said to you. For example, "You feel I am not spending enough time with you." This clarifies what you have heard and shows the other person you understand the criticism. If the criticism is vague or uncertain, it may be helpful to ask the other person to be more specific.

Take a deep breath and then take a moment to decide if the criticism is accurate or useful. If so, you may want to ask for specific instructions, suggestions, or alternatives. For example, "What are your ideas or suggestions about how we can spend more time together?"

If you feel the criticism is unjust, you may want to share your feelings with the other person so they will know the effect it is having on you. For example, "You may have misunderstood what happened," or "I'm feeling bewildered by your statement because I just spent the weekend with you."

Don't always take criticism personally. Consider the source of the person criticizing you. Is this his typical style of communicating? Don't try to get even; live beyond an eye-for-an-eye mentality and try to respond kindly or with gentle humor. When the criticism is angry, it's okay to calmly but firmly say, "I'm not comfortable about the way you are talking to me right now."

Other ways of dealing with criticism might be to say, "You have a point," or "I see your point," or "You could be right," or "I hadn't thought of it that way, let me think about this and get back to you later."

Your assignments for this chapter:

1. Practice using "I" messages.

2. Ask a friend to help you monitor your communication to see if you are becoming more assertive.

3. Consider taking assertiveness training at your community school.

4. Read books on assertiveness or personal power.

5. Practice centering by taking a deep breath and being in touch with your thoughts and feelings.

6. Don't take criticism personally.

7. Examine criticism carefully to see if it is accurate and to determine what you can learn from it.

8. Start a monthly optimism chart or graph, and each day work on becoming more optimistic.

9. Gratitude:
   - I am grateful for choices and personal power in my life.
   - I am grateful for constructive criticism.
   - I am grateful for positive thoughts.

10. Memorize and repeat these affirmations:
    - I enjoy being balanced and centered at all times.
    - I feel more powerful and in control of my life.
    - I handle confrontations with ease.
    - I am creating happiness, love and success for myself.
    - I am dissolving barriers to my self-expression.
    - My communication is more honest and open.
    - I am becoming more optimistic each day.
    - I am a positive and powerful person and I am using my power to make good decisions in my life.

15
Using Humor as a Healing Tool

*A merry heart doeth good like a medicine:
but a broken spirit drieth the bones.*

—Proverbs 17:22

This Chapter's Messages:
The Many Advantages of Humor

Humor is the ability to look at the ridiculousness in our own lives and find something to laugh about. It won't eliminate the problem, but it will help overcome the effect. Life is at least as funny as it is sad. Humor can stop a misunderstanding from escalating and ease tension when no other strategies will work. It can soothe hurt feelings and create a sense of well being.

Even the Old Testament book of Proverbs recognized the value of humor and laughter in healing. Life can be too serious.

During elections for student body officers, a young high school student told his peers, "If I am elected to office I will buy everyone a puppy." Not everyone wants a puppy, and receiving one would not be my choice. If I could buy something for everyone who is depressed or has the "blues," it would be a giggle doll. When my husband was having serious arrhythmia with his heart and was concerned about his own mortality, I felt helpless because I couldn't change the predicament. While shopping and searching for something to cheer us up, I suddenly heard the most refreshing and infectious giggle, just like a happy baby. I chuckled. Who doesn't like to hear a baby laugh? It was a giggle toy called "Swing Me." It giggled when you pressed its hand, and when you swung it in the air it said,

"Whoopee." Of course, I bought it; the giggling entertained and gladdened us. The grandchildren loved it.

Erma Bombeck had a wonderful way of seeing humor in everyday life. She once wrote, "We sing, 'Make a Joyful Noise Unto the Lord' while our faces reflect the sadness of one who has just buried a rich aunt who left everything to her pregnant hamster."

Time Changes Perceptions

Time has a way of changing our perception. My husband grew up in a small town. As a young boy, he was fascinated by the trains that ran through the community. Once, upon a very frosty morning, he and his group of friends were crossing the railroad tracks when a friend dared him to place his tongue on one of the rails. As many adventurous ten-year-olds might do, he accepted the dare, and immediately his tongue was frozen stuck to the rail. No matter how hard he tried he could not free his tongue from the track. Anticipating the arrival of the train, the group grew panicky. One boy suggested warm water, but they were not anywhere near warm water. Another piped up, "Maybe we should pee on it!"

At that suggestion, my husband began protesting, but was only able to utter undistinguishable sounds and flail his arms at the boys who were about to urinate on his tongue. Finally one of the boys ran to a near-by home and returned with warm water. Meanwhile the whistle of the approaching train echoed in the distance.

At the time, his situation wasn't funny at all. Now, as he shares it with his children, it's quite humorous.

I like this story about a secretary: "I see you were last employed by a psychiatrist," said the employer to the applicant.

"Why did you leave?"

"Well," she replied, "I just couldn't win. If I was late to work, I was hostile. If I was early, I had an anxiety complex. If I was on time, I was compulsive."

Laughter releases physical tension. It combats feelings of anger or fear, and it helps us feel in control of our response to stressful events. An ability to find humor can give us a sense of perspective on our problems.

I still like the story of the man who approached the desk in the doctor's office and when asked why he was there, replied, "I have shingles." The nurse took down his name, address, and medical insurance number and asked him to have a seat. Fifteen minutes later another nurse came out and asked why he was there. "Shingles," he said. She took his height, weight, complete medical history and asked him to wait in the examining room.

Half-hour later, a third nurse arrived and asked why he was there. "I have shingles," he repeated. She took his blood pressure, and a specimen and then told him to take off his clothes and wait for the doctor. The doctor arrived twenty minutes later and asked him what he had. The man answered, "Shingles."

The doctor asked him where they were and the man answered, "Outside in my truck. Do you want me to start working on the roof today or tomorrow?"

If You Can Laugh, You Can Survive

Bill Cosby says, "If you can laugh at it, you can survive it." Often, we are not able to control events in our external world, but we can control how we view these events and our emotional response.

A study at the College of William and Mary in Williamsburg, Virginia, has shown there is a unique pattern of brain-wave activity during the perception of humor. Humor perception involves the whole brain and serves to integrate and balance activity in both the brain's hemispheres. Electroencephalograms were recorded on subjects during the humorous experiences. At the beginning, the brain's left hemisphere began its analytic function of processing words, then most of the brain activity moved to the frontal lobe, which is the center of emotionality. A few moments later the right hemisphere's synthesis capacity joined with the left's processing to "get the joke." Milliseconds later the activity spread to the occipital lobe, the sensory processing area of the brain. Increased fluctuations in delta waves reached a crescendo of activity and crested as the brain "got" the joke and the person started laughing.

Almost nothing in the universe represents greater wonder or complexity than the human brain. In his book, *Head First*, Norman Cousins said, "If the brain of an average fifty-year-old person could be fully emptied of all the impressions and memories it has stored, and recorded on tape, the length of the tape would reach to the moon and back several times."

In the 1960's Cousins was hospitalized by a rare, crippling disease, and when he learned it was incurable he decided to dwell on becoming well again. Every day he watched humorous films or videos—the Marx Brothers, Candid Camera reruns, old Laurel and Hardy pictures and other slapstick features. He said that ten minutes of genuine belly laughter gave him two hours of pain-free sleep. For a time, his fatal cellular disease was reversed and he spent the last 12 years of his life at the University of Los Angeles Medical School in the Behavioral Science department exploring the therapeutic effects of laughter and humor in healing the body. Cousins believed that faith, hope, laughter, and the will to live are biochemical factors that can actually help combat serious disease. Today there are scientific studies attesting to that relationship.

Cousins spent considerable time collecting jokes, stories, cartoons and humorous antidotes. One joke he told: "Honey, if I weren't rich, would you still love me?" Wife's reply, "Of course I'd love you—I'd miss you, but I'd love you."

Cousins said, "Humor used at the proper time can help break the "panic cycle" that so often accelerates a patient's illness or state of mind. Laughter can broaden the focus and diffuse the intensity of negative thoughts . . ."

When his best friend was hospitalized with a life-threatening disease, instead of sending flowers, he made her a loose-leaf book of laughs stuffed with cartoons, classic witticisms, and personalized homemade jokes.

The Physical Results of Laughter

Laughter boosts endorphins, endorphins lift depression. Mirthful laughter helps strengthen the immune system, muscles and bones, the respiratory system, the central nervous system, and the cardiovascular system. Dr. William Fry, a Stanford University psychiatrist, says "Twenty seconds of laughter can double the heart rate during that time period, just like jumping on an exercise bike."

Next time you're in distress, flex your funny bone. It might help.

Children have a wonderful ability to find humor in life and make adults laugh. When my daughter, Jennifer, came into the house all dressed up for work, my three-year-old granddaughter quipped, "Jennifer, you're wearing your Cinderella dress."

The *Reader's Digest* says that laughter is the best medicine.

Recently I attended a wedding reception and was surprised to find I was the first guest there. A young man with a video camera greeted me and insisted that I state my name and give advice to the newly married couple. Hesitant to appear before the camera and stumble over my words, I pleaded for a few minutes to collect my thoughts. Finally, after much deliberation, I stepped cautiously before the camera and delivered a profound message to the bride and groom, then slipped into the reception line and reflected on the wise advice I had just given.

Pictures were still being taken of the wedding party, but the bride's parents were nowhere in sight. Suddenly, an older couple crowded into the wedding line and stood next to the groom's parents. Curious about whom they might be, I turned to the woman behind me and asked about the couple.

"They're the bride's parents," she answered.

"Is this the Courtland/Allan wedding?" I asked.

"This is the Loveland/Mitchell wedding," she laughed.

Right night, wrong wedding. Eventually I found the right wedding.

I like the following quips:

"When I die, I want to go peaceably in my sleep like my grandfather did, . . . not screaming and kicking like the passengers in his car."

"Some people place faith in a rabbit's foot, but remember, it didn't do the rabbit any good."

"Dear God, So far today I've done all right. I haven't gossiped or lost my temper. I haven't been greedy or grumpy or nasty or selfish or overindulgent. And I'm very thankful for that. But, in a few minutes, I'm going to get out of bed—and from then on, I'm probably going to need a lot more help. Amen."

Humor can be helpful even in a crisis. While my husband was in the hospital after they removed his kidney because of kidney cancer, he had congestive heart failure, and was having a tough time. Wanting to try anything to cheer him up, I took my battery operated fairy godmother's wand to the hospital. A beautiful young woman with long flowing blond hair, dressed in white clothing, and resembling an angel, stepped onto the elevator. I sensed her sadness and gently asked, "Do you need a fairy-godmother's wand?" as I waved the blinking wand toward her.

Tears rolled down her cheeks as she nodded in the affirmative.

As she stepped off the elevator, I reached out to comfort her and listen. She had two small children and was going through a traumatic divorce. Her mother was in the hospital for kidney failure and had been waiting for a kidney transplant for five years. "My mother is tired of fighting for her life. She wants to give up and die, but she just barely turned fifty. My father is dead, and I don't want to lose my mother. I feel so hopeless," she cried.

"Why don't you take my fairy-godmother's wand," I suggested. "You can return it to my husband's room later this evening."

Several hours later my husband was delighted to see a beautiful angel, dressed all in white, walk into his room carrying a fairy-godmother's wand. "This was great," she said, as she handed me the twinkling wand. "Mother loved the wand. She even laughed. We took turns waving it around the room and granting wishes for the nurses that were coming in and out. She now has hope and the will to live."

Your assignment for this chapter:

1. Start collecting jokes, funny stories, cartoons, and antidotes to put in a loose-leaf binder. Make copies so that you can pass them on to friends or relatives who are ill of depressed.

2. Ask your friends or relatives to send or save humorous short stories, cartoons and antidotes for you.

3. Find something to laugh about at least ten times a day.

4. Learn to laugh at yourself.

5. Gratitude:
- I am grateful for humor in my life.
- I am grateful for a sense of humor.
- I am grateful for Walt Disney.

6. Memorize or read these affirmations daily:
- I have a great sense of humor.
- Love and laughter are joyous parts of my life.
- I have enthusiasm to live life to the fullest.

Everyone smiles in the same language.

16
Fighting Chronic Fatigue Syndrome, Epstein-Barr Virus and Candida

*Faith is the assurance of things hoped for,
and the conviction of things not seen.*

—Hebrews 11:1

A Search for Healing of Chronic Fatigue

For months I had been ill, but couldn't understand why. After trying repeatedly to find a doctor that could diagnose what was wrong with me, I finally found a doctor who dealt with Chronic Fatigue Syndrome. He was in internal medicine, and had specialized in CFIDS (Chronic Fatigue Immune Dysfunction Syndrome) because his own son had the disease. Since he was practically the only physician in the city who understood CFS at that time, his practice was overwhelming. He eventually became so burned out he left private practice and went into research, but not before he helped me. I remember feeling so ill, depressed, and worthless, that I said to him, "If I can't get better, I want to die."

The important thing I want you to know is that I did get well, and you can also. Don't ever give up hope.

When I first became ill, I had my blood checked in a live cell analysis at a health food store where they discovered a lot of parasites in my blood stream. A live cell analysis involves taking a sample of your blood and magnifying it many, many times. They have a monitor that looks like a television screen and you can see your own blood cells. I could see tiny little parasites swimming around in my blood.

When I approached my physician at the time, I was told that it wasn't possible to have parasites in your blood, and he told me I was probably just suffering from stress or depression. He referred me to a counselor who thought Prozac was the panacea for every depression. After one week on Prozac I was more depressed than ever, by the second week I was suicidal. When I called the counselor, she suggested I double the dosage. There was no way I was going to double the dosage and feel twice as suicidal.

I also knew that CFS attacks the central nervous system and that while stress contributed to my depression, I needed to get physically well. I immediately stopped taking the Prozac, and within a few days the suicidal feelings went away. I never went back to that therapist.

After that, my doctor referred me to a psychiatrist, who on the first visit and without any testing whatsoever, wanted to put me on a MAO inhibitor. He suggested my symptoms were psychosomatic (all in my head). I walked out of his office and felt sorry for his patients. He had the empathy of a brown recluse spider.

Please don't misunderstand me, there are many wonderful physicians and counselors available to help you, but it's important that you take responsibility for your own health and check out the side affects of medication. My concern, is the number of clients I've seen who are taking one of the major anti-depressant drugs and now have life altering side affects such as rapid weight gain, and for many women, a loss of sexual desire that causes serious problems with their marriage.

My physician recommended an antidepressant that caused tardis dyskinesia (swelling of the tongue because of an allergic reaction to a medication). When I discussed this with him, he discounted the swelling and suggested I increase the dosage. I didn't at the time, but later increased the dosage and had terrible side effects. My tongue became thick and heavy and I couldn't enunciate my words properly. My mouth was constantly dry. When I tried to sleep, I felt like I was doing a continuous round of backward somersaults. My life was so out of control, I felt like I might die and knew I could if I stopped fighting to get well and just stayed in bed. I stopped taking the medication and the symptoms went away.

Perhaps you can understand why I favor natural remedies for depression over prescription medications. If you are depressed and are not on medication, find a doctor or an alternative health care practitioner that works with natural remedies. Consider taking with you the list of natural remedies that my physician gave me for depression. It is listed in chapter five of this book.

Every morning I felt like I was pushing a ten-thousand-pound truck off my body just to get out of bed. Walking two blocks exhausted me for the whole day. I could not hurry; there was no energy to hurry. Still, I got up every morning and went to work because I was committed to the young people I was working with and I could do counseling sitting down. While at work, I lost myself in their problems and rarely thought about myself. After work, I went home and fell into bed.

One day, while at a conference I ran into an old friend I hadn't seen in four years. She didn't recognize me. Then she said, "Pat, what's happened to you? Your aura—your light—it's gone."

At times I would start feeling better and was elated that my health and energy was returning. Then I would overdo, and suddenly I would be right back at square one, as ill as ever.

Then, by some miracle I found Dr. Beales, the doctor who finally helped me. He gave me medicine to fight the candida that was in my blood stream and had permeated my cells. I made drastic changes in my diet. Within two weeks I started to improve. Still, I wasn't completely well.

It wasn't until I started using the remedies for killing parasites in the blood, that were suggested by Dr. Hulda Clark, in her book, *The Cure for Any Cancer*, that I started feeling better. But the real healing process came during the summer when I had time off from work and I went to visit my daughter in California.

Even though I was exhausted, I managed to drive to California by myself, making short stops along the way. In Las Vegas, I stayed overnight with friends.

Renewal in California

Before I left for California, I was at church one day when the electrical power suddenly went off and it was very quiet. A still small voice inside my head kept saying over and over, "You need to leave, you need to leave." My doctor had been encouraging me to take a vacation or somehow get away from the stress at home, but I felt I couldn't leave my responsibilities.

Somehow the escape from our five difficult teenagers, (who weren't bad teens, they were just all pulling in different directions) and the pressure of trying to sell my house, turned into a spiritual journey I hadn't anticipated. I listened to cassette tapes of scriptures, and religious and classical music during the fourteen hours of driving.

My daughter lived only fifteen minutes from the ocean, so each day I sat on the beach or slowly walked barefoot through the sand and felt the waves nip at my feet. Somehow the ocean energized me and recharged my spiritual batteries, but more than anything there seemed to be a spiritual connection between me and the many people I met in California.

Encountering Kindred Spirits

One evening I met a wonderful black family from Ethiopia. Four older sons were there with their mother. Even though she couldn't speak English, we seemed to connect spirit-to-spirit. Her sons translated and she asked if I was religious. She invited me to her son's home in Garden Grove, where she was visiting. They gave me the address,but it wasn't an invitation I thought I would accept because I didn't know my way around Southern California.

The next day, after meeting my daughter for lunch, I heard an inner voice say to me, "I want you to take the mother roses." "Roses?" I questioned. "I'm on a budget. What about carnations?" "No! Roses," was the direct reply. Then inwardly I started complaining, "It's hot, I'm tired, and I don't know how to find Garden

Grove." Then came the nudge from the inner voice, "Okay, next time you want something . . . ." "You win," I said as I pulled into the turn lane to try and find Garden Grove.

In the island in the middle of the road, next to the turn lane, a young man was selling flowers. He shoved them into the open window of my car—roses—! I glanced down to see a half dozen red roses right under my nose. "How much?" I asked. "Eight dollars, he replied. I quickly fumbled for my wallet, "I only have three, will you take a check?" "I'll take the three dollars," he said. I shook my head in amazement.

When I finally found the small, but immaculate house in Garden Grove, the mother was strolling outside with her son and baby granddaughter. She was delighted to see me and said, "We know that God sent you to us last evening." I did not understand. She cuddled and adored the roses, then embraced me affectionately.

Like old, long-lost friends, we talked for several hours while her son translated. Her husband had died shortly after my first husband died, and she raised ten children alone in Ethiopia. Then, somehow an overpowering feeling told me that in the heavens, our husbands knew and associated with each other. And she knew it too.

During my short stay in California, I met thirty people that I felt a spiritual connection to, and in each case, we each felt closer to God after our conversations. I felt an overwhelming love for each of these people. There was an amazing synchronicity, but even more amazing was the physical and spiritual healing that came into my life. I was now on the road to complete remission.

Chronic Fatigue Symptoms

There are several types of CFIDS. One is the slow-building type that makes fatigue a natural part of your life. You are always tired. My chronic fatigue hit as suddenly as a lighting bolt and was almost as devastating. I had symptoms of exhaustion. At times I was unable to sleep at all, and at other times I could sleep all day. I experienced short-term memory loss, muscle pain, joint pain, a sore throat, lymph-node pain, severe depression, difficulty concentrating, bloating, fever, chemical sensitivities, weight gain, earache, and shortness of breath. My equilibrium was off. The bottom of my feet hurt so badly I could hardly bear to walk on them.

While there are probably many causes of CFIDS, candida and parasites in my blood were the main causes of my disease. My present physician, who also studies nutrition and alternative healing, believes that candida is the cause of eighty-five percent of the cases of CFS. Tish Mecham, a bio-kinetist who has worked with several thousand individuals with Chronic Fatigue, believes that candida is the cause of most CFS episodes. The book, *Natural Healing*, by Dr. James Balch, states that sixty percent of the people infected with EBV also have candida and he recommends they drink at least eight glasses of water a day and add some form of acidophilus to their diet. I also had Epstein-Barr, all kinds of digestive and bowel problems, and a fragile immune system.

No one knows the exact cause of CFIDS, and everyone who contracts it is different. Still, I would recommend eliminating stress. Begin with the deep breathing from the left nostril (by blocking the right nostril) for five minutes every time you feel stress. Learn to scan your body for stress and learn how to let go of it. Turn to the chapter on stress management and yoga and practice breath of fire. Do it in the morning before you have eaten, or in the evening three or four hours after your evening meal. At first you may not have the energy to breathe rapidly and deeply for very long, but start with a few minutes a day and gradually work up to as much time (15 to 30 minutes) as you can comfortably handle. Take it easy and don't overdo. This is a wonderful way to detoxify the body.

Recommended Readings Related to Chronic Fatigue

I think that toxins in our body contribute to illness. There are some books I want to recommend. Two of them are very old, but worth reading. They were both written by Dr. Bernard Jensen. The first is *Doctor-Patient Handbook*, dealing with the reversal process through eliminating diets and detoxification, and the second is *Tissue Cleansing Through Bowel Management*. *The Yeast Connection*, by Dr. Crook has a questionnaire to help determine if you have intestinal candida, and it discusses remedies and the right diet. *Digestive Wellness*, by Elizabeth Lipski, is an excellent resource. She recommends a biological, rather than medical approach because, she says ". . . it saves money and works better. In one study . . . a nutritional approach costs $2,000, compared with $10,000 for a medical approach." However, there are now some medical doctors that have embraced alternative and nutritional health care.

Other books include, *Enzymes and Enzyme Therapy*, by Anthony J. Cichoke, D.C., and *A Holistic Protocol for the Immune System*, by Scott Gregory. *Feet First*, by Laura Norman, is an excellent book about foot reflexology, and *Touch For Health*, by John F. Thie, D.C., is a new approach to restoring your natural energy. There are also additional books available. Search your library and Internet resources for more information that might be helpful to you. Keep looking for positive answers.

Check for Parasites

Not everyone will have intestinal parasites, or parasites in their blood, but it's worth checking it out. A medical doctor will have to check for intestinal parasites, but to check for parasites in your blood by live-cell analysis, you will probably have to contact a naturopath or a good reliable health food store in your area that either schedules this type of blood test or can refer you.

Hulda Clark recommends a remedy in her book, *The Cure For Any Cancer*, for getting rid of parasites and intestinal flukes. It includes Black Walnut Tincture, Wormwood in capsules, and Cloves. Work with a health-care practitioner to determine the right dosage for you. She also suggests that you not use any products with propyl alcohol or anything with the word, "prop," because parasites thrive on propyl. Good luck on that issue, because almost all cosmetics have isopropyl alcohol. When I discovered I had liver cancer, I stopped using hair spray, perfume, some shampoos, rubbing alcohol, most cosmetics, mouthwash, white sugar, and carbonated beverages. A friend, who is a physician, said to me, "Now, I guess you're going to have to live in a tepee by the side of an alpine stream to avoid all of the toxins in our environment."

Dr. Clark states that propyl alcohol accumulates in the liver and is not detoxified. However, the liver gets rid of some of the alcohol by dumping it through the bile ducts into the intestine where it encounters sometimes millions of fluke (parasite) eggs. Dr. Clark states her belief, "Since propyl alcohol is a solvent, I think it dissolves the shells of the eggs and lets them all hatch!" This is her theory, though she agrees it needs more research.

After I took Cloves, Wormwood, and Black Walnut tincture for three months, the parasites in my blood were gone and I began to feel healthy again. Also, Ginkgo was very beneficial in helping me regain my memory.

Recommendations for Fighting Epstein Barr Virus and Candida

Tish Mecham, author of the book, *Bio-Kinetic Testing For Health*, has given me permission to share her recommendations for eliminating Epstein-Barr virus and candida.

For EBV, avoid fats because they plug the liver and the liver is a vital organ in fighting EBV. Some foods high in fats are cheese, ice cream, chocolate, salad dressings, red meats, pork, deep-fried foods, shell-fish, chips, pastries, shortening, french fries, donuts, butter, etc.

Avoid potatoes, green peppers, and eggplant, because these foods seem, to be a breeding ground for the virus.

The Epstein-Barr formula includes one quart of white wine. Bring the wine to a boil for seven to ten minutes. Remove from heat and add one tablespoon of powdered wormwood (you can purchase this from health food stores that sell herbs in bulk). Let cool, and strain if desired. Store in refrigerator. Muscle test for dosage that is right for you. Most adults take four tablespoons a day until they are feeling significantly better. This is a rapid remedy to kill the virus.

In addition, there are herbs that kill the EBV. I recently had a flare-up of EBV and took Echinacea and Burdock Root to halt the virus. It took about three weeks to kill the EBV.

Cleansing the Colon and Intestinal Tract

Dr. Bernard Jensen, author of *Tissue Cleansing Through Bowel Management*, said, "In the 50 years I've spent helping people to overcome illness, disability and disease, it has become crystal clear to me that poor bowel management lies at the root of most people's health problems. In treating over 300,000 patients, it is the bowel that invariably has to be cared for before any effective healing can take place."

The greatest healing power comes from within out. This is based on "Hering's Law of Cure." It states, "All cure starts from within out and from the head down and in reverse order as the symptoms have appeared."

Basically, this means that when you start on an elimination of wastes from your body or a detoxification program, you likely will feel worse for a short period of time as the toxins are released. Symptoms of previous illnesses may appear for a short duration, but they will soon disappear. If you are quite ill, it is recommended that you detox slowly. After eliminating toxins and wastes from your body, your health will improve dramatically.

There are five elimination channels or systems in the body: skin, lymph, respiratory, kidneys, and the bowel. Bernard states, "The body depends on a clean bowel. The cleanliness of any tissue, i.e., kidney, stomach, brain, depends upon what is found in the bowel."

Because the modern-day diet consists mainly of refined and processed foods and lacks fiber, the majority of people today have the type of constipation where old, hardened feces stick to the walls of their colon and don't pass out with regular bowel movements. Intestinal parasites and candida thrive in this filthy environment.

Adequate nutrients are not absorbed when hardened feces stick to the colon walls. This is why some people are always hungry.

According to Robert Gray, author of *The Colon Health Handbook*, "Autointoxication is the process whereby the body literally poisons itself by maintaining a cesspool of decaying matter in the colon. The toxins released by the decay process get into the bloodstream and travel to all parts of the body. Every cell in the body gets affected, and many forms of sickness can result." Autointoxication weakens the entire system.

Gray says, "The cause of autointoxication is putrefaction within the intestinal tract. Putrefaction is a process of decay in which foul odors and toxic substances are generated." Ideally, daily bowel movements should have very little or no putrefactive odor. "There is a close relationship between body odor and putrefaction within the intestinal tract."

Robert Gray recommends a low-mucoid diet to improve the health of the colon and intestinal tract. Nonmucoid material moves through the body quicker than mucoid material. Gray claims, "The bowels tend to move two to three times per day when the intestines and colon are in a nonmucoid condition. You will never attain superb health before all of the old, hardened feces within your body have been dissolved and removed."

Mucoid-forming foods include all dairy products from cow's milk, Gray says. This includes, milk, skim milk, cheese, butter, cottage cheese, yogurt, and whey. Also, all flesh foods—meat, fish, fowl, and eggs. Soy beans are the most mucoid-forming of all plant food.

"Vegetables and fruits are virtually free of any mucoid-forming activity. They are nature's purest foods," Gray says.

Gray recommends mucotiptic herbs or other agents to loosen, soften, or dissolve hardened, stagnant, or impacted mucoid in the body. I will list a few of these herbs here: acacia gum, aloes, grapes, oatstraw, olive oil, red clover flowers, spaghetti squash, spirulina plankton, chickweed, and zucchini. In addition, he says psyllium husks are unsurpassed at removing loosened material.

Nature's Way makes a natural herbal stimulant called "Naturalax 3."

Dr. N.W. Walker, author of *Fresh Vegetable and Fruit Juices*, suggested carrot and spinach juice for cleansing the colon. Use one part spinach to three parts carrots. Spinach contains oxalic acid and this stimulates peristalsis. Don't eat cooked spinach because it can cause oxalic crystals in the kidneys. I like the spinach/carrot combination because carrot juice also detoxifies the liver.

Dr. Diane Farley-Jones, a general practitioner in Alpine, Utah, who also does homeopathy, treats many clients with CFS. She prescribes 5-HTP (hydroxytryptophan) for depression. She also gives Vitamin B12 injections because this helps normalize imbalances in red blood cells.

According to John Morgenthaler, who wrote the book *5-HTP*, 5-HTP is the natural alternative to Prozac. It is a natural plant extract that raises serotonin levels in the brain without the adverse side effects of drugs. There is evidence that 5-HTP has been helpful for relieving depression; alleviating anxiety, panic, and obsessive-compulsive disorder; reducing the pain and frequency of migraine attacks; alleviating the pain and discomfort of fibromyalgia; improving sleep; and suppressing appetite and losing weight.

Because 5-HTP is a naturally occurring substance, it can be purchased at most health food stores. Not everyone needs to increase their serotonin levels, so check with a health practitioner and do not take it with other prescriptions without checking with your physician.

Dr. Barnett Salzman, an orthomolecular psychiatrist in Fresno, California, recently discussed with me Omega-3 oils as a means of treating depression. He said that recent research has shown some remarkable results with salmon oil in addressing depression.

In some of my readings, it has been suggested that lack of essential fatty acids can contribute to CFS.

Clustered water might be something else you would like to consider. Dr. Lee Lorenzen, who developed or replicated clustered water, has a Ph.D. in Nutritional Biochemistry and is a licensed clinical nutritionist. Many years ago, his wife became very ill with an immune dysfunction that was so serious she was bedridden for three years. Desperate to help her, Dr. Lorenzen began adapting various resonant techniques to water. According to the doctor, over time, with much research, experimentation, and prayer, he was able to replicate and stabilize the water which is present in high concentrations when we are born. At birth, trillions of young cells are filled with this "clustered" water. "Even the DNA in each of our Cells, which determines how we grow and what we look like, is folded around a core of this remarkable water."

"As we grow, our clustered water becomes physically bound to other molecular structures and unable to move freely through the cell walls. Our body contains approximately ten million cells. The water that sustains them is called clustered water. Unlike tap or rain water, Clustered water has a particular characteristic which allows it to pass freely through cell walls, delivering oxygen, nutrients, protein chains, enzymes, and it removes the toxic buildup that accumulates in the cells."

Dr. Howard Wolin, who is a professor at Northwest University and has a private practice in Chicago, Illinois, said, "I am a physician who works with advanced nutrition to help patients improve their overall wellness and detox from multiple toxic stressors. Clustered water is, in my opinion, a highly valuable adjunct in this work. Its capacity to effect changes at intracellular levels enables the body to more efficiently detox and hydrate the cells and, in my opinion, enhance cellular communication and cellular function. I recommend it very highly."

I have personally used clustered water and found that it does increase my energy. One caution: if you are going to use clustered water and you are quite ill, start slowly. Remember the reversal process I wrote about when you start detoxifying the body. At first you may feel worse, but gradually you will improve. It takes time to get rid of toxins in the body. For most people there are no side effects, but others may take two to six weeks to remove toxins from their body. Instead of drinking the recommended 16 ounces a day, start with two ounces and gradually increase to the 16 ounces.

For more information on clustered water, call 1-800-864-2362. The name of the company is Cellcore.

Main Homeopathic Remedies for Chronic Fatigue Syndrome

There are three main homeopathic remedies for CFS, and these also work for EBV and Mononucleosis. Homeopathics are safe for everyone and have no side affects. Homeopathic health practitioners prescribe according to an individual's temperament or constitution.

In choosing a homeopathic remedy, a health practitioner will find the description of the person's disposition at the present time, and prescribe according to that temperament. Homeopathy is discussed in more detail in Chapter 17 of this book.

First, *Gelsemium:* this remedy will treat an individual who has a weakness on a physical, mental, and emotional plane. The weakness can sometimes include paralysis. The main symptom is a flu-like illness. It can be accompanied by diarrhea and drooping eye-lids.

The emotional clue to this remedy is fear—fear of the future, or apprehension about getting well, and a loss of hope. This can include fear of flying, going to the dentist or doctor, or taking a test. Frozen in fear typifies this individual and they frequently seem emotionally paralyzed.

The second main remedy is *Calcarea Carbonia* (made of the clam shell—these people tend to clam up): these people are over-worked, overwhelmed, with a strong sense of duty. They are very responsible and their breakdown comes from over-work. They bite off more than they can chew. Physically, these people tend to be flabby or overweight. Also, they have lots of fears and phobias that control their lives, especially about their health and severe diseases.

The third main remedy is *Mercuius Sol:* it is made of non-toxic mercury, hence the name, mercurial, which means impulsive or introverted tendencies. Their moods seem to change with the Mercury (weather). They also have many fears and suspicions. The main symptom is difficulty with the mouth, teeth and gums, accompanied by bad breath. Often, they have a metallic taste in their mouth and frequently have night sweats.

"Diet is crucial to building the immune system and conquering CFS," states Dr. Michael Murray, N.K., of Seattle, Washington. "A healthy diet avoids 'empty' foods low in nutrients and high in sugar and fat." In the book, *Alternative Medicine*, he points out how important it is to eliminate all allergic foods and to drink eight to ten glasses of pure water daily.

Murray also suggests that magnesium deficiency may be a problem for CFS patients. "According to a recent study, twenty people with CFS were compared to twenty healthy volunteers; the CFS patients' magnesium content of the blood was shown to be lower. In another study, patients were given intramuscular injections of magnesium. Eighty percent of those receiving the magnesium had reduced symptoms and improved energy."

Olive leaf capsules (purchase at a health food store) and Pau d' Arco tea also fight viruses, bacteria, and candida. In addition, "Essential Oils" have a powerful effect on wiping out bacteria and viruses. For more information call 1-800-763-9963 and ask for a free brochure or cassette tape on essential oils.

Mecham's yeast-cleansing formula should be taken at bedtime. Mix 8 ounces of water with one tablespoon liquid clay or one teaspoon powdered clay. Take one acidophilus capsule. Break one capsule caprylic acid and one acidophilus capsule into the mix. Add one heaping teaspoon psyllium husks and mix in a blender. Drink quickly, then follow up by drinking an additional eight ounces of water.

The book, *Alternative Medicine*, quotes Bill Wesson, D.D.S., of Aspen, Colorado, who says that "Chronic Fatigue Syndrome can be due, at least in part, to amalgam fillings in the teeth, which contain over 50 percent mercury, a highly toxic substance." Wesson cites a case of a female patient who suffered from CFS for over twenty years and who had tried a variety of treatments which all proved useless. He removed fourteen amalgam fillings in her teeth and replaced them with non-toxic material and her CFS symptoms were alleviated.

Some health practitioners believe that neurological aberrations in the body can affect the immune system. Each cell in our body has a memory. When there is an aberration, this memory is unable to communicate and tell the body how to heal. Emotions are traditionally thought of as being normal functions of human beings, which normally pose no neurophysiological problems. Occasionally, emotional trauma causes a neurological pattern which does not resolve itself. Health practitioners use the Neuro Emotional Technique to help release the aberrations and help the body heal. It is usually a chiropractor who uses N.E.T. to normalize imbalance by changing physiology using a structural correction or adjusting the body. I've been to the training and have been impressed with the results. For more information on health practitioners in your area that use N.E.T., call 1-619-944-1030 or write N.E.T., 524 Second Street, Encinitas, CA, 92024.

Additional Sources of Help in Fighting CFS and EBV

To obtain further help contact:
CFIDS Association, Inc.
P.O. Box 220398
Charlotte, North Carolina 28222-0398
1 (900) 988-2343
1 (704) 365-9755

The official book of the CFS Network is:
Hope and Help For Chronic Fatigue Syndrome, by Karyn Feide. (New York: Fireside Books, 1990.)

Recuperate Patiently and Positively

Be cautious about exercise because in some cases, exercise can worsen the symptoms. If you are able to walk, that's great, but don't overdo. Dr. David Bell, author of *Curing Fatigue*, suggests that as your symptoms begin to subside, you use this rule of thumb: "Exercise gently, to the point where the aching and flu-like symptoms that characterize CFIDS flare up—then stop. . . . Going beyond this can bring on a relapse."

Even though you are ill, take your pain and do something positive with it—help others, give joy to the world. Write notes or make telephone calls to the elderly and shut-ins; or read or make tapes for the hearing-impaired. Find something you love to do that doesn't take a lot of physical energy. Connect with your higher power, read scriptures or religious or other uplifting books. Listen to inspiring music and positive tapes. Listen to Bernie Seagul's healing meditations. Seagul is the doctor who wrote, *Love, Medicine, and Miracles,* and said he was such an ugly baby and little child that other kids were constantly harassing him. When things went wrong in his life, his mother would say, "It's okay Bernie, God is redirecting your path, and something good will come of it."

Watch sunsets, listen to birds, smell the flowers, love others, and love yourself. Above all, know that this too will pass. "The grand essentials to happiness in this life are something to do, something to love, and something to hope for," wrote Joseph Addison. Never give up hope for recovery.

Increase Your Emotional Altitude Each Day

Measure your own progress towards recovery by making a graph with the numbers one-to-ten on the left hand side of the page. Write the number "ten" at the top of the page and the number "one" at the bottom. Number "one" will represent the lowest level of your fatigue and depression. At the top of the page, write the dates for each day of the next month. Strive to find some way to diminish your level of depression and fatigue by at least one number every day or week. Imagine that you are in an elevator and you are on the third floor, the goal is to emotionally bring yourself up to the fourth floor. If you're on the fourth floor, climb up to the fifth level so that each day you're increasing your emotional altitude.

Each morning make a list of what you can do to recuperate and to be less depressed today. Flip back through the pages of this book and find ideas you know might help you.

Measure Your Goal Accomplishment

In the evening, write your goals for the following day in your daily log. How do you plan to reach your goal? If it's an enormous aspiration, break it into small, workable chores that you can bite off a little at a time. Explain in detail your plan to accomplish your goal. An ounce of planning is worth a pound of work.

Each evening, write down if you accomplished your goal. If you reached your goal, write down why you think you achieved your goal. If you did not accomplish your goal, write down why you did not realize it. Don't set yourself up to fail by choosing unrealistic goals.

Your assignments for this chapter:
1. Pray or meditate each day. Abraham Lincoln said, "God is the silent partner in all great enterprises."

2. "Ask and it shall be given you: seek and ye shall find . . . ." (Matthew 7:7)

3. Research books on Chronic Fatigue.

4. Breathe in healing, blow out illness. Repeat this many times a day.

5. Visualize yourself being bathed in white light that is healing your body, mind, and spirit.

6. Breathe in happiness, blow out depression.

7. Learn about detoxification and good nutrition, and apply this knowledge in your life.

8. Gratitude:
   - I am thankful for healing in my life.
   - I am grateful for a higher power that reaches out to heal me.
   - I am grateful to be getting better.
   - I am ecstatic about having more energy.
   - I am grateful for a positive attitude.
   - I am grateful for the journey of life.
   - I am grateful to be happy.

9. Memorize or read these affirmations daily:
   - I face each day with renewed energy and hope.
   - Each day my body is healing, and pure love radiates through me.
   - The cells in my body are being renewed and energized.

- I have a sense of humor.
- Laughter and humor are a part of my everyday life.
- I sleep peacefully each evening.
- Each new day is a bounteous blessing.
- I am learning to love and embrace myself as I am.
- All things are working together for my highest good.
- I am in touch with my Higher Power.
- The divine spark within me is creating miracles in my life.
- Wherever I am, God is, and I feel His love.
- Divine light and love radiate through me and to everything around me.

17
Homeopathic Remedies for Depression

Truth which men have sought, and sought in vain . . .
This undiscovered treasure, yet has lain
Buried not deep, but just below the ground
By the Wise Hand that wished it to be found.

—Hahneman, quoting Stellert—1700's

Homeopathy Defined

Homeopathy is a holistic form of medicine that is used to help the body heal itself. Hippocrates understood and used the basic precepts of homeopathy, but homeopathy as we know it, was founded in the late 1700's by a German doctor named Samuel Hahneman. Disillusioned by the rampant spread of disease and medical practices of his day, he gave up conventional medicine and discovered that a substance that can produce symptoms of illness in a well person can, in minute doses, cure similar symptoms of disease. The word, "homeopathy" means treating like with like.

According to Dr. Norman Shealy, author of *Alternative Medicine*, "Homeopathic remedies are completely safe for everyone from babies, children, pregnant women and to the elderly, and in all states of health. Homeopathy remedies can be safely used in the home and are not very expensive." However, homeopathy does not always work for everyone that tries it. Medical students in Britain have asked that homeopathy be included in their training.

Treating the Whole Person and Each Person Individually

The fundamental philosophy behind homeopathy is treating the whole person and remembering that each person is an individual with different characteristics and needs, and must be treated as such.

Shealy writes that "Homeopaths believe that a person's temperament or constitution is made up of inherited and acquired, physical, mental and emotional characteristics and that these can be matched to a particular remedy that will improve their health, no matter what their illness."

A homeopath studies a person's temperament, personality, the foods they like or dislike, and their emotional and physical responses before they prescribe anything. Remedies are usually prescribed one at a time.

Patients should see some change within a few days of taking the treatment. Remedies work quickly and in most cases can be taken with other medications or herbs. However, some substances such as highly perfumed cosmetics, minty flavorings, strong smelling household cleaners, and aromatherapy oils have the ability to counteract the homeopathic remedies and should be avoided.

Understand that a remedy is prescribed according to an individual's constitution or mental, physical or emotional characteristics.

When my daughter went through a devastating divorce, she was weepy, felt out of control, unassertive and unsure of herself.

After consulting with a health professional, she started taking the homeopathic remedy, Pulsatilla (the wind flower), with great results. She developed an inner power and confidence that sustained her throughout the ordeal.

Homeopathic Remedies for Various Types of Depression

Dave Card, who is a homeopathic practitioner, prepared the following list of homeopathic remedies for depression and has given me permission to share them with you. It is a condensed list of some of the major remedies and in no way contains all the remedies for depression. Each remedy describes a certain type of constitution. For example, Aurum Metalicum would be the remedy for the deep depression a person has when dealing with financial loss.

Aurum Metalicum (a homeopathic prepared gold—highly diluted): This is the number one remedy for depression: symptoms include, suicidal feelings with despair, extreme insomnia—nothing but a bright sunny day will lift their spirits or hopes, they form strong attachments to people, and suffer in silence with no consolation. While grieving, they experience heartache, reminiscing, and sighing. They tend to be "proper" people (oftentimes business men).

Natrum Muriaticum (homeopathic prepared salt) is the second major remedy for depression. These people suppress emotional pain, are sentimental with flatness, and have watery eyes. They are depressed at grief or loss, and sigh a lot. They make statements such as "I've already worked things out." They deny depression and live in silence and accept no consolation.

Staphysgsgria: These people have suppressed anger, grief, putting self down (I will never amount to anything), won't talk, and feel worthless. They have the triad of guilt, worthlessness, and depression. This remedy is often used for victims of all kinds of abuse (physical, sexual, verbal). After taking the remedy, these people often choose to leave an abusive or destructive relationship.

Ignatia: It tends to be a remedy for women who feel in conflict, and are confused, disappointed, and perfectionists. Ignatia is the most widely used remedy for depression as a result of grief from losing a loved one in death or loss of a romantic interest. These people tend to sigh constantly. Sighing is a "keynote" to the remedy.

Alumina: This is often used for depression in the elderly where there is severe constipation and confusion. These people cannot hurry, it only makes them more confused.

Kali Carbonicum: These people tend to be rigid and strict parents. When their depression is severe, they sit and stare at the wall and have a blank look that is almost catatonic.

Natrum Sulphuricum: These people have often suffered a brain injury. Their liver tends to be impaired from overwork and they can be suicidal to the point that they must restrain themselves. It is their duty to their family that keeps from committing suicide. There is a weariness about them and they have a strong sense of duty.

Tubercullinum: These people are the travelers. They visit exotic places, but feel emptiness inside. They feel unfulfilled, reach out, and nothing is there. Also, there is a physical respiratory weakness.

Silcea: These people are delicate, determined, and feel fragile—like they have a weakness of the mind. They are usually physically cold.

Phos Ac: These individuals have a deadness inside from overwork. Mentally, they feel shut down. Other symptoms come from grief or loss of a loved one.

Sepia: This describes the woman who feels depressed because of hormonal problems, especially after taking birth control pills or artificial hormones. They feel dead inside and don't want anyone to touch them and often reject their husbands.

Pulsatilla: Most often, this describes women who are weepy, moody, and whining. These women desire companionship and are the peace-keepers at any price—usually at the expense of their own happiness. They will stay in unhealthy relationships. They are the "givers" and often feel abandoned. Abandonment is their big issue.

Lachesis (made of snake venom that is perfectly safe and highly diluted): They are extremely talkative, strong-willed, self-pitying, and can be mean-spirited. They tend to strike out at others and are verbally abusive and aggressive. Depression sets in around their monthly menstrual cycle. Most of their physical complaints are centered on the left side of their body.

The potency for each remedy is usually 30 C, taken once a day or as needed. When the correct remedy is taken, symptoms should improve immediately. Dr. Shealy said, "In acute conditions, doses should be taken every half hour to begin with, to a maximum of ten doses." When the symptoms improve, the interval between doses should be 8 to 12 hours for two or three days at the most. Take the remedies only for as long as you need to and if a remedy doesn't work within a short period of time (about a week), stop taking it. Consult a health practitioner about what might be best for you.

For more information, contact The International Foundation for Homeopathy in Seattle, Washington, at 206-324-8230. For additional reading, the book, *Homeopathic Psychology*, by Dr. Philip M. Bailey, is an excellent resource that covers personality profiles of the major constitutional remedies.

*Greatness is not found in
possessions, power, position or prestige.
It is discovered in goodness, humility, and character.*

Bibliography

Balch, James F., M.D., & Balch, Phyllis A., *Prescription for Natural Healing*, Garden City Park, New York: Avery Publishing Group, Inc., 1997.

Bell, David S., *Curing Fatigue*, Emmaus, Pennsylvania: Rodale Press, 1993.

Bhajan, Yogi, & Khalsa, Shakti Parwha Kaur, *Kundalini Yoga*, Los Angeles, California: Time Capsule Books, 1997.

Chichoke, Anthony J., D.C., *Enzymes & Enzyme Therapy*, New Canaan, Connecticut: Keats Publishing, Inc., 1994.

Clark, Hulda, Ph.D., *The Cure For All Cancers*, San Diego, California: ProMotion Publishing, 1993.

Cousins, Norman, *Head First*, New York: Dutton, 1989.

Crook, William C., *The Yeast Connection*, Jackson, Tennessee: Professional Books Inc., 1996.

Diamond, John, *Your Body Doesn't Lie*, New York: Warner Books, 1994.

Dyer, Wayne, *Manifest Your Destiny*, New York: Harper/Collins, 1997.

Glasser, William, *Choice Theory*, New York: Harper/Collins, 1998.

Gray, Robert, *The Colon Health Handbook*, Reno, Nevada: Emerald Publishing, 1991.

Gregory, Scott J., *A Holistic Protocol for the Immune System*, Joshua Tree, California: Tree of Life Publications, 1995.

Jensen, Bernard, *Doctor Patient Handbook*, Escondido, California: Bernard Jensen, 1976.

Jensen, Bernard, *Tissue Cleansing Through Bowel Management*, Escondido, California: Bernard Jensen, 1981.

Jovanovic, Pierre, *An Inquiry Into the Existence of Guardian Angels*, New York: M. Evans, 1995.

Lipski, Elizabeth, *Digestive Wellness*, New Canaan, Connecticut: Keats Publishing, 1996.

McWilliams, *You Can't Afford the Luxury of a Single Negative Thought*, Los Angeles, California: Prelude Press, 1995.

Mecham, Tisha, *Bio-Kinetic Testing for Health*, Sandy, Utah: Living Dreams, LLC.

Morgenthaler, John, & Lenard, Lane, *5-HTP, The Natural Alternative to Prozac*, Petaluma, California: Smart Publications, 1998.

Morter, Ted, *Dynamic Health*, Niles, Illinois: Tru-Vantage International.

Pfeiffer, Carl C., *Nutrition and Mental Illness*, Rochester, Vermont: Healing Arts Press, 1987.

Pfeiffer, Carl C., *Mental & Elemental Nutrients: A physician's guide to nutrition and health care*, New Canaan, Connecticut: Keats Publishing, 1975.

Ritchie, George, *Return From Tomorrow*, Grand Rapids, Michigan: Chosen Books, 1978.

Robertson, Joel, *Natural Prozac*, New York: Harper/Collins, 1997.

Schiffer, Fredric, *Of Two Minds: the revolutionary science of dual-brain psychology*, New York: Free Press, 1998.

Siegel, Bernie, *Love, Medicine, and Miracles*, New York: Harper & Row, 1986.

Shealy, C. Norman, *Alternative Medicine*, Rockport, Massachusetts: Element Books Inc., 1996.

The Burton Goldberg Group, *Alternative Medicine: The definitive guide*, Tiburon, California: Future Medicine Publishers, 1997.

Thie, John F., D.C., *Touch For Health*, Pasadena, California: T.H. Enterprises, 1987.

Whitaker, Julian, *Guide to Natural Healing*, Rocklin, California: Prima Publishing, 1994.

Index

A

A Holistic Protocol for the Immune System—127
Abou Ben Adhem—92
Acidophilus capsule—134
Addison, Joseph—136
Affirmations—22, 26, 38-40, 43, 50, 51-56, 64, 67, 73, 87, 95, 102, 112, 119, 137
Alumina—141
Alternative Medicine—134, 139
Amino acids—20, 28-30
An Inquiry Into the Existence of Guardian Angels—48
Anger—15, 16, 21, 25, 27, 41, 54, 57-64, 65, 73, 82, 107, 110, 141
    symptoms of—58
Anxiety—11, 19, 20, 24, 27, 29, 34, 63, 65, 76, 78, 80-82, 114, 131
    symptoms of—80
Applied kinesiology—63
Arginine—28
Arousal-Depressed Personality—37
Assertive message—108
Assertiveness—103-108, 112
Aurum Metalicum—141
Autointoxication—129
Awfulizing—70

B

B complex vitamins—30, 34
B12/folic acid shots—30
Bailey, Dr. Philip M.—143
Balance—109-110
Balch, Dr. James—126
Beales, Dr.—123
Bell, Dr. David—135

Benzodiazepine—26
Bifidium bacterium—36
Bio-Kinetic Testing For Health—31, 128
Bio-kinetic testing—31, 128
Biokinesiology—31
Black Walnut Tincture—127
Blood sugar—34
Braza, Jerry—83
Breathing, deep—76-77, 110, 126
Burdock Root—128

C

Caffeine—33, 38, 80
Calcarea Carbonia—133
Calcium—34, 81
Campbell, Don—42-43
Candida—35, 36, 118, 123, 126, 128, 129, 134
   symptoms of—35
Caprylic acid—36
Carbohydrates—28, 33, 34, 38
Card, Dave—140
Cerebral allergy—37
CFIDS Association—135
Chamomile—81
Chamomile Tea—19
Choice Theory—58
Christensen, Dr. Larry—33, 34
Chromium—34
Chronic fatigue—25, 36, 90, 121-138
   symptoms of—125, 134, 135
Cichoke, Anthony J.—127
Citrus seed extract—36
Clark, Dr. Hulda—123, 127, 128
Cloves—127
Clustered water—131-132
Co-enzymes—34
Colon—129
Coolidge, Calvin—101
Cooper, David—82
Copper—37

Cortisol—25
Cosby, Bill—115
Cousins, Norman—116
Criticism—111
Crook, Dr. William C.—36, 126
Curing Fatigue—135

D

Deep breathing—16, 33, 76-77, 80-82, 84, 87, 126
Depression—13-17, 19-22, 23-43, 46, 47, 57-59, 61, 75, 81, 82, 91, 101, 117, 122, 123, 125, 131, 136, 139-143
  causes of—25
  defined—23-24
  Dysthymia—24
  Manic-Depressive Disorder—24
  Melancholic Depression—24
  symptoms of—23-25, 141
  triggers—26
Diabetes—25
Diamond, Dr. John—331
Diflucan—36
Digestive Wellness—127
Digitalis—26
Doctor-Patient Handbook—126
Dopamine—25, 27, 28, 37. 38
Dr. Carl C. Pfeiffer—19, 34, 37
Dr. Whitaker—20, 29
Dyer, Dr. Wayne—52, 90, 91
Dysthymia—24

E

Echinacea—128
Elimination channels—129
Emerson, Ralph Waldo—41
Endocrine disorders—25
Epstein-Barr Disease—25
Essential Oils—134
Exercise—16, 21, 26, 31, 34, 63, 76, 78, 79, 87, 135

F

5-HTP—131
Farley-Jones, Dr. Diane—131
Fear—63, 65, 69-73, 82, 104, 110, 115, 133
Feet First—127
Feide, Karyn—135
Finding Serenity in the Age of Anxiety—72
Fresh Vegetable and Fruit Juices—130
Fry, Dr. William—117

G

GABA—20
Garlic—36
Gelsemium—133
Gerzon, Robert—72
Ginkgo Biloba—30, 128
Gita, Bhagavad—91
Glasser, Dr. William—58
Goals—42, 45, 55, 79, 80, 136-137
God (higher power),
   angry with—16, 59
   availability of—72, 89-95, 129, 137, 138
   closeness to—72, 85, 125, 138
   help and blessings of—13, 16, 41, 48, 50, 63, 72, 92, 94, 95, 98
   His will—49-50, 94, 100, 136
   relationship to—53, 89-95, 136, 138
   thanking—26, 38, 51, 64, 73, 85
Goldenseal—36
Gratitude—22, 26, 36, 43, 50, 56, 64, 67, 73, 85, 87, 95, 101, 112, 119, 137
Gray, Robert—129, 130
Gregory, Scott—127
Guardian angels—48-50, 95
Guilt—14, 16, 21, 26, 59, 63, 65-67, 141

H

Hastings, Robert J.—99
Head First—116
Hering's Law of Cure—129

Histadelia—37
Histapenia—37
Histidine—28
Hoffer, Dr. Abraham—36
Homeopathic Psychology—143
Homeopathic remedies—20, 30-31, 133-135, 139-143
Homeopathy defined—139
Hope and Health For Chronic Fatigue Syndrome—135
Hops—81
Humor—16, 46, 54, 111, 113-119
Hyperthyroidism—25
Hypoglycemia—33, 34, 37
Hypothyroidism—25

I

I Messages—105
Ignatia—141
Insomnia—23, 35, 80, 81, 141
   Maintenance insomnia—80
   Morning insomnia—80
   Sleep onset insomnia—80
Isoleucine—28
Intestinal Tract—129

J

Jensen, Dr. Bernard—126, 129
Johimbine—30
Johnson, Peter E.—48-49
Jovanovic, Pierre—48

K

Kali Carbonicum—141
Khaslsa, Shakti Parwha Kaur—83
Kinesiology Muscle Testing—31-33
Kundalini Yoga, the Flow of Eternal Power—83
Kunin, Dr. Richard—38

L

L.72 Anti-Anxiety formula—20
L-tyrosine—29, 37

L-tryptophan—30
Lachesis—142
Lactobacillus acidophilus—36
Lady Slipper—81
Laughter—117
Leucine—28
Lipski, Elizabeth—127
Li-zyme Lithium—30
Lorenzen, Dr. Lee—131
Love, Medicine and Miracles—136
Lysine—28

M

Manganese—34
Manganese gluconate—34
Magnesium—30, 81
Manic-Depressive Disorder—24
Manifest Your Destiny—91
McWilliams, Peter—70
Mecham, Tisha—31, 126, 128
Melancholic Depression—24
Menninger, Dr. Karl—20
Mercuius Sol—133
Methionine—28, 29
Mindfulness—83
Morgenthaler, John—131
Morter, Dr. Ted—51
Murray, Dr. Michael—134
Muscle
   pain—125
   relaxation—78-79
   testing—31-33, 128
Music Miracles—42

N

Natrum Muriaticum—141
Natrum Sulphuricum—142
Natural Healing—126
Natural Prozac—37
Negative self-talk—69

Neuro Emotional Technique—135
Neurotransmitters—25, 27, 29, 75
Niacin—19, 30, 81
Norepinephrine—25, 27, 28, 37, 38
Norman, Laura—127
Nutrition—16, 19, 26, 27-38, 76, 127, 132, 137
Nutrition and Mental Illness—37
Nutritional hypoglycemia—37
Nystatin—36

O

Of Two Minds—22
Olive Leaf capsules—134
One-to-ten scale—106
Optimism—76, 86, 87, 109, 112, 148

P

Parasites—127-128
Passion Flower—81
Paul D'Arco tea—36, 134
Personal power—37, 103-112
Pessimism—109
Pfeiffer, Dr. Carl C.—19, 34, 37
Phenylalanine—28, 29
Phos Ac—142
Phosphorous—34
Positizing—70
Potassium—34
Progressive relaxation—78-79
Propyl—127
Proteins—28
Psyllium—36
Psyllium Husks—134
Pulsatilla—140, 142
Pyroluria—37

R

Relaxation, progressive—78-79, 81
Renoir—99
Return From Tomorrow—21

Robertson, Dr. Joel—37, 38
Role playing—107-108
Roosevelt, Eleanor—70

S

Salzman, Dr. Barnett—131
Satchidananda, Swami—93
Satiation Depression—37
Schiffer, Dr. Harvey—22
Schizophrenias
　biotypes of—37
Seagul, Bernie—89, 136
Self-Test—104
Sepia—142
Serotonin—25, 27, 28, 37, 38, 131
Shealy, Dr. Norman—139, 140, 142
Siberian Ginseng—30
Silcea—142
Skullcap—81
Socrates—94
St. John's Wort—30
Staphysgsgria—141
Stress management—85, 86, 126, 148
Substance abuse handout—71-72
Sugar problems—33
Suicidal feelings—15, 16, 19-22, 24, 29, 34, 57, 122, 141, 142
Support systems—11, 16, 26, 45-50, 59

T

Tanalbit—36
Tardis dyskinesia—122
The Colon Health Handbook—129
The Cure for Any Cancer—123, 127
The Golden Present—93
The Need to Trust—93
The Old Frog—100
The Station—98-99
The Yeast Connection—36, 126
Thie, John F.—127
Threonine—28

Tissue Cleansing Through Bowel Management—126, 129
Touch For Health—127
Train station—52, 63, 98, 99
Trust—67, 69, 71, 73, 93
Tubercullinum—142
Tyrosine—28, 37

V

Valerian Root—81
Valine—28
Victim language—108
Visualization—41, 76, 85, 91, 137
Vitamin B3—34, 81
Vitamin B6—25, 37, 81
Vitamin B12—25, 81, 131
Vitamin C—19, 30, 34

W

Walker, Dr. N. W.—130
Wesson, Bill—134
Whitaker, Dr. Julian—20, 29
Winfrey, Oprah—55
Wolin, Dr. Howard—132
Wormwood—127

Y

Yoga—16, 26, 83, 85, 126
You Can't Afford the Luxury of a Negative Thought—70
Your Body Doesn't Lie—31

Z

Zinc—34, 36

About the Author

Pat Webb received a bachelor's degree in Mass Communications and a master's degree in Educational Psychology from the University of Utah. She is a Ph.D. candidate in Nutrition and Natural Healing at Clayton College of Natural Health (CCNH). She is a lecturer on nutrition, depression and mental health issues, stress management, and her favorite topics, "Optimism" and "Healing Your Spirit."

She is a Licensed Professional Counselor (LPC) in private practice, the President of the Utah Mental Health Counselors' Association, a high school counselor in Utah's Granite School District, a member of the Association of Mormon Counselors, and a nutritional consultant. She has done drug and alcohol counseling, family therapy, grief therapy, marital therapy and individual counseling. For four years she served on the board of the Salt Lake County Alcohol and Drug Program.

Always an advocate for youth, she also volunteered at the Youth Detention Center and did family therapy for Salt Lake County Youth Services Center. She was a coordinator of the Women's Education Resource Center where she implemented a self-sufficiency program for single parents and displaced homemakers. She was the crisis counselor, instructor, and mentor for four-hundred women.

With a life-long interest in helping people, Pat helped sponsor Asian refugees, housed unwed mothers, and after the death of her first husband started a support group for single women. Thirty years later, the group is still meeting.

She has written articles for *This People Magazine*, the *Deseret News*, and was a zone editor for *Spectrum* and the *Midvale Sentinel*.

In addition to the extensive community and professional service she has rendered, she has been active in her church. For five years she worked as a substitute seminary teacher. She has been a guide at the Beehive House, served as a visiting teacher, primary teacher, stake family history coordinator, spiritual living teacher, ward newsletter editor, Relief Society President, counselor in the Relief Society, and an MIA teacher.

Pat is the mother of seven children and seven step-children. She currently has eight grandchildren and one great-grandson. Her hobbies include gardening, dancing, and experiencing the warmth and love of grand-children.